Strong Woman, Stronger Assets

By Jessica Weaver

Strong Woman, Stronger Assets

ISBN-13: 978-1546498353

ISBN-10: 1546498354

Cover design by Miladinka Milic

Dedication

To all the women out there working to live the life they want and showing other women the way.

I dedicate this book to my amazing and supportive husband, who found out I was writing it a day after I told him I was pregnant. He spent an hour and a half on the phone with my publisher to get reassurance I could write the book I've always wanted to publish and that I could get it done before the baby was born. He always supports my crazy ambitions, listens to my endless talks about helping women, and is my constant sounding board for advice. I have so much respect and love for him, and for what he does every day to protect those around him. I wouldn't be where I am today without his constant guidance and support. Even though I don't tell him how thankful I am that he is in my life, I do say thank you to God every day for sending me Eric. Love you!

Two other people, I would like to mention since I wouldn't have written this book without them are my parents, Alix and Dan Foran. As you will note throughout this book, they are a huge influence on my life and in what I do. I admire and respect my mom for being strong enough to recreate a life for herself after having a rough childhood. She is my reason for helping more women find their strength not only with their money but with their lives. I thank my father for bringing me into the world of finance, to find a way to help people, and for giving me the flexibility to discover a method to love what I do and focus all my energy on it.

And lastly, to my bundle of joy, who will be born in September. People thought I was crazy when they found out I was pregnant and writing a book while continuing to work, including my husband at first. But you gave me the motivation to get this book written on a deadline, and you also have given me more reasons to continue down my path of helping women. I hope to be a role model in your life, a pillar of strength when times get tough, and to be there to celebrate your victories. We don't know whether you are a boy or a girl right now, but we will know by the time this book is published, so stay tuned until the end when you will get a surprise!

Table of Contents

Foreword

On September 9, 2016 I had a call with a young woman I had met through LinkedIn. From the moment our conversation began, I was excited to know more about her.

Here I was speaking to a woman with drive, passion, desire and so much heart to help women that it seemed to spill out of her. But it wasn't success that she was after, it was a relentless **yearning** to make a difference with women and their finances.

This woman, of course, was Jessica Weaver, the author of this book, *Strong Woman, Stronger Assets.*

Jess and I hit it off right away because we share a mission of empowering women to make better financial choices so they can improve the quality of their lives. This is a driving force behind my business and compels Jess to do what she does as well.

Over the last nine months that I've gotten to know Jess while having her in my business mentorship program, I've come to understand how truly determined she is to making an impact on women's lives. I've witnessed her unstoppable commitment to create impactful change and watched her grow and stretch as a person and leader.

As a Business Coach and Trainer for women with a background as a CERTIFIED FINANCIAL PLANNER™ practitioner, I have worked with hundreds of women personally and understand the challenges women like you go through.

Managing your day-to-day finances, making the "right" financial decisions, investing your money, protecting your family and your income — **none** of this is taught in school.

Yet, the choices you make when it comes to your money affects <u>every single area</u> of your life including your emotions, your relationships, your material possessions, your quality of life, your career decisions and so on.

But how can you avoid potential mistakes that could lead to a life of financial hardship or even unnecessary struggle?

Whether it's being in debt, feeling overwhelmed with financial choices, overcoming financial devastation, dealing with the aftermath of a divorce, or simply having confusion about how to grow your money and set yourself up for retirement, this book can help you get on the path to success.

Imagine sitting at a coffee shop with Jessica and hearing such engaging and captivating stories that you feel **compelled** to make a change in your own life.

Imagine knowing exactly what next steps you need to take and feeling like the issues that used to *plague* you, now feel so simple and easy to tackle.

This is could be your experience when reading this book.

Jessica mentions in the book how money is a taboo subject. She points out how it can be changed to a "no big deal" conversation that you can feel **comfortable** being a part of.

For example, for many, creating a financial plan may seem tedious, overwhelming, daunting, or even unnecessary. However, in chapter 5, Jessica shows you how to design a simple financial plan that's catered to your lifestyle, so that you'll actually follow it. Jessica <u>emphasizes</u> the importance of having a plan, regardless of your financial situation because it helps give you confidence and get in control of your money, while relieving stress or burden.

There are so many books out there that overpromise and under-deliver, leaving the reader confused and uncertain. This book <u>clearly</u> and <u>efficiently</u> unfolds the information with story after story of inspiring women.

If you follow Jessica's guidelines step-by-step included at the end of each chapter, **you can** potentially start to create the life you desire.

You can feel empowered and excited to take on your money challenges and can become confident from having the support of a mentor by your side.

One of the most important takeaways from this book is to identify your <u>motivating</u> <u>factor</u>, your reason for change. Jessica walks you through this to uncover your "why" and what specifically drives you to take action, so you can mold your future.

Please take this book seriously, it can possibly change your life.

-Robyn Crane

Speaker, Trainer & Business Coach for Women #1 International Best Selling Author of *Make More Money, Help More People.*

Chapter 1: Let Me Introduce Myself

"Women have been trained to speak softly and carry a lipstick. Those days are over." ~Bela Abzug

I want us to start our journey together by sharing something very honest and personal with you. I've often said it is better to start a relationship with honesty, so here goes: I used to be very unhappy at work. Sound familiar? I'm sure you can name at least 10 people who don't like their job. Why was I unhappy? Well, I didn't like what I was doing because I didn't see the impact I was making on people's lives. And this is only the first flaw or secret I will share with you about myself; there will be more. But first, let me take you back to the beginning, so you'll have a better idea of how I got to the place of being unhappy, bored, and frustrated with my job.

I grew up in a family of four with amazing parents and the best older brother you can ask for, plus some fur babies along the way. We were always a close, tight-knit family, and I hold a lot of great memories close to my heart. Our family was extremely busy like any family nowadays, with sports games, vacations, work, and school. My father is a financial advisor and has been for the past 35 years. He has a successful firm, but as any small business endures, there were some bumps in the road along the way. At one point, when I was a little girl, I remember declaring: "I will never have anything to do with the stock market when I'm older!"

Why would a little girl ever make such a ridiculous statement? Because I was sick of the stock market's performance being the reason for the number of birthday and Christmas gifts we'd get or being the predictor for why my father was in a bad mood. Not that he was in a bad mood often. To give you an idea of my father, he is one of the greatest men on this planet, and I am lucky enough to have him as a parent. He is the most generous man I've ever known, and never expects anything in return. In fact, every birthday and holiday, he yells at us not to get him anything while he gives, gives, and gives.

Fast forward to when I was a little older and in high school. I started to see my father's job in a different light. He would explain how his job was similar to being a coach who helps people obtain their financial goals and dreams. Well, that sounded pretty neat to me. If someone wanted to get to retirement, he could help. If a couple wanted to send their children to college, he could show them the way. So, I started thinking how incredible it would be to help people the way my father has been able to. Which leads me to the next chapter of my life. I went from a little girl with pigtails, who wanted nothing to do with investments to a financial advisor helping women and investing in that "terrible" stock market.

I joined my father's financial advisory firm right after college, and I worked there during my summers to learn about the industry. After speaking with my father numerous times about my future and dream career, I decided to join his firm after completing my college education. Once my cap and gown were off, I got right down to business and passed all my insurance and securities licenses that first summer. I joke about studying more that summer than I did during all of college. I then proceeded to earn my CFP designation, which usually takes people two to three years, but I was on the fast track. I took all the courses and passed the exam within a year and a half. Again, this comprised more studying than I ever did in college.

Through some learning humps, we started growing our business and had some early success. We brought in more referrals, ran some retirement seminars, and were getting people to their goals. Still, something seemed to be missing for me, but I was in such an early stage of my career, I didn't give it any thought. It's like when you are starting something new; you really want it to work out great, so you might ignore some warning signs. *It just has to work out*, right?

Life was pretty good, so I continued on my path for a few more years. I was making some money and working with my family, so I didn't have much to complain about. I was making an impact on people's lives by helping them save for their financial goals. It was nice showing people how to save for their children's college, for their retirement, or to get out of debt. But I had an emptiness inside me, and I started getting more and more bored at work. To make the situation worse, I felt as if I were failing my father…who was tickled pink about working with his two children. He bragged about it to everyone!

To say the least, I was floundering at my current job and felt so very stuck. Do you know that feeling? Where you dread going to work every day? I felt absolutely terrible about it, too. Here was my father, who had put a big bet on me, and I wasn't happy. We would always put our clients first and do the right thing for them. Not for us. Still, it seemed like I was selling products to our clients instead of transforming their lives. Maybe I'm a bit delusional, but I've always thought I was put on this earth for a bigger purpose.

And then something changed when I went to my first Raymond James Women's Conference, and I felt so inspired. Seeing other women advisors doing important work and experiencing such success with their creative ideas, moved something inside me. I came back from the trip grinning from ear to ear, then went to work that first Saturday and put a plan in place. It was scary and overwhelming to start a new focus in my career, but I knew it would be worth it. I knew if I didn't make a change, I would either stay stuck or have to change careers. With these thoughts, I committed to my new work. Within weeks, I held my first Transitioning Women's workshop and even served chocolates and mimosas. A month later, I held a yoga event just for women, all because I wanted to get women more excited and involved with their money and finances. It was freeing to know my mind and heart were aligned with my career and my career goals. My passion started to really kick in when I hosted these unique and fun women's events. During the summer of that same year, I did a markets and martinis party, a Not-Your-Father's-Advisor's type of event. I was rejuvenated and excited about work again. It was amazing.

My passion shifted again when I decided to write a blog, called *Not Your Father's Advisor*. With so much unrelatable information out there, there was such a need. None of the content women have available to them is interesting, and definitely, none of it is geared toward them. I have so much fun with the blog, and it has become a new way to get women talking about money. When they are more open about their financial situations with each other, it makes it all worth it. My blog gained more steam when I started to see my views increase and due to the tremendous feedback from my readers. I was more inspired and ecstatic each morning going to work, and I was even working extra hard at night and on the weekends. I was finding my way to something bigger than just me and my happiness; it was about changing women's lives. To give them a way to experience a transformation and to lead them toward feeling stronger and more independent and confident with their money.

And finally, it seemed the universe had put everything in line for me when I met my mentor and coach, Robyn Crane, from a simple LinkedIn message. It's mind-blowing how taking such a small action can change your world. She showed me the impact I can have on women's lives and how that impact will only breed more of my own happiness. The more lives I change, the more thankful and happy I become, which only fuels my passion and desire to transform more women's lives. It's so rewarding to see women get more involved with their money and finances and to, dare I say, have some fun with it! I like to think this book will be the piece that enables it all to click into place when it comes to understanding your relationship with money, and that your world will start shifting in the same way it has for me.

Because it isn't about the money, is it? More money isn't going to fix our money issues. It is about finding our happiness and putting ourselves on a path to get enjoyment out of our lives. Earning more money is a nice perk, but it isn't everything. My mission is to show women they can have the lives they want and deserve, and how to not only get there but how they can learn to stay there.

As I worked with more and more women, I saw them take a tough time in their life and change it into a new opportunity. It was fascinating to help them gain control and clarity over their money and their life. I felt such satisfaction at giving them the confidence in their choices from knowledge, education, and most importantly, having a plan. So, while all the events, blog postings, and newsletters are a blast for me and help my creativity, the real joy and desire to keep working, comes from seeing the transformation of the women who work with me. This is why I get up every day, excited for work. It's why I work almost every weekend, and why I won't stop hustling until I change more women's lives.

This spark inside me is what fuels my desire to mentor and coach women, to continue writing my blog and this book, and to never stop because it is bigger than just me. And every woman I meet and work with reminds me of just that. When I push for your transformation, it is because I know you can do it and you deserve to do it for your life. It's tremendous to see the impacts that occur from gaining control and clarity over your money. It really does affect our lives in more ways than you think. Money alters our everyday life whether we want to acknowledge it or not. I've seen from numerous women an astonishing difference in how they value themselves after we've worked together. As they start changing their beliefs to match what they want and deserve in their life, they automatically change the value of their own life. They elevate the value of their life, and the ripple effect can be remarkable because the rest of the world starts to take notice. And you will start changing your money habits to grow your money to match your life's value. Then the people around you will start valuing you more, and you will probably start to earn more money. At least, this is what I've witnessed in the women around me and in the women who are my clients.

Remember this saying as you embark on your new adventure to uplift your life:

It takes 4 weeks for us to notice a change within ourselves.

It takes 8 weeks for our family and friends to notice.

It takes 12 weeks for the rest of the world to notice.

But

It only takes 1 day to say we are enough; we are worth the change and the hard work. Our lives are worth it!

It works the opposite way as well, doesn't it? When we see our bank accounts at a new low, how do we feel about ourselves? When we see debt piling up, how do we value ourselves? Our self-esteem tends to plummet along with our bank accounts. So, take some time to decide which way you want your self-esteem to go and which way you want your bank account to go. If you were asking me, I'd say the higher, the better and reach for the stars. Remember the title of the book, **Strong Woman, Stronger Assets** since they go hand in hand. As strong women, we embrace the change because we know we can handle it and the outcome more than outweighs the work to get there. To breed the beliefs in you, I will share some real-life stories of women who have been where you are, and who are now in control of their money and their lives. They conquered their money fears, slew their old money stories, and have come out stronger and more independent than ever before.

One woman was brought into my life right at the beginning of writing this book, and she reminded me exactly what I stand for when we started working together. A huge motto of my life is "everything happens for a reason," and all the women who've come into my life to help are there for a reason. This is her reason for coming into my life: she was only taught one thing as a young girl, how to be a wife first and then a mother. She was brought up to **not be** a breadwinner, to **not** have a career, and to be kept in the dark about money. During our strategy session, she explained how only her brother had been pushed to work, to get good grades, and go to college. She was supposed to only be a mother and a wife. She was never allowed to control the family's finances or money. When she was married, her husband controlled all the expenses and didn't let her in on any of the financial discussions. It is no surprise these limiting ideas of how women are supposed to be stayed with her even beyond her divorce. I can't begin to imagine how that would make me value myself. I'm going to go out on a limb and say I'd feel horrible and have a very low self-worth.

Because of her low self-worth from her childhood, she has a recurring problem with debt and being paid too little for her value. When she was a wife, her husband took care of the finances. Unfortunately, he wasn't any better at it than she would have been. The marriage ended with very little money, and she had to find a way to raise five children alone and on a school secretary's salary. Now, she has been divorced for over 20 years, and she has never had a full year without debt. To create the retirement she wants, she knows she needs to start changing her mindset around money. Since she'd received an inheritance and found herself in more debt, she knows more money won't solve her money issues. She needs help changing her beliefs about what she can have for her life and consequently, what her behaviors are concerning money.

No women should feel they don't have a voice in the family's finances, that their questions may sound stupid, or that they will never have the life they want. Take a leap of faith with me or borrow my belief that you can have the life you want and the life that you deserve to have. You owe it to yourself to at least see if it's worth it. All it takes is a decision to start living for your self-worth and to elevate your life. This woman is doing exactly that now. Her new mantra is that she deserves to live debt free and have a bountiful retirement. What will be your new money mantra?

A mantra is a saying you repeat in meditation to stay connected in the moment. We need a money mantra in our lives to stay grounded in our beliefs when we are tempted to sway from them. You can start a new chapter in your life by reading this book, and with the new chapter comes a new mantra to live by. I call this redefining moment in your life, your new money mantra. There will be times when you are exhausted, stressed, and frustrated beyond belief, and during those times, it is key to remember your money mantra. What are you working toward? Your new life, your new money mantra.

You are here for a reason, and I don't want you to let the tough times you've gone through define the rest of your life. Let's take action together and turn the page to start your transformation. Throughout this book, I hope you gain more beliefs and confidence to keep your momentum going, so you can take more actions. To make sure you do, I will have bonuses in various chapters with clear steps outlined, because none of the information is worth it if you don't know what to do with it.

Here is your first bonus exercise:

Have you ever thought of something you really wanted, visualized yourself with it, and then it happened?

Go to a quiet place, turn the lights down low, and sit comfortably. Not so comfortably you fall asleep, but sit up straight with your hands resting on your thighs. If you'd like, play some soft and relaxing music.

Empty your mind of your to-do list. Imagine it vanishing just for five minutes. It will be there when you open your eyes, but for now, it has simply floated away, out of reach.

Once you have quieted your mind, at least somewhat, think about your perfect day. What will it look like? Will you sleep in a little, get up and go for a nice walk to find it's perfectly beautiful out? You get to do only the things you love, whatever they are. Picture yourself doing it. Are you on your dream vacation? At a job you love? On your first day of retirement? Really be in the moment. What are your surroundings? Use all your senses. What are you seeing, smelling, hearing, tasting, touching? What are you feeling?

What are your emotions? Do you feel happiness, relaxed, energized?

Now that you've pictured it, do you think you'll start changing your beliefs and behaviors to get yourself there? I hope so, and if you think so, too, turn the page to start the process.

Chapter 2: The Story of My Grandmother and Other Strong Women

"A strong woman loves, forgives, walks away, lets go, and perseveres…no matter what life throws at her." ~Unknown

I grew up during the Girl Power Movement, and truly believed I was going to be the first woman to play in the NBA. Then the WBNA was created, and I couldn't believe how cool it was. Look how far women have come in sports! Sorry hubby, but even my college basketball team could beat yours. Now being in the working world, it is remarkable how many women are company executives and CEOs. We have a long way to go still, but we are gaining momentum. More and more girls see their moms able to tackle the roles of mom and career woman, and they get inspired. Even daughters of working moms tend to earn 25 percent more when they start their careers[1].

I'll take that 25 percent bonus anytime. So yes, we are on our way to having it all!

It is no surprise how much I admired all the strong women in my life growing up. My own mother came from a terrible childhood only to break the odds and build such an amazing childhood for me and my brother. She decided early on that she wasn't going to let her childhood dictate her future. And it isn't like my grandmother admired her daughter for taking such a stance on her life.

—

[1]Carmen Nobel, "Kids Benefit From Having a Working Mom," http://hbswk. hbs. edu/item/kids-benefit-from-having-a-working-mom, (May15, 2010).

She tried to break her down and belittle what she had done with her life pretty often. And for my mother to be a better daughter to her mother than my grandmother was as a mother, is successful in my book. Even though life was tough on my mom in the beginning, she knew what she wanted for her life. She had the clarity of what was important to her and acted to create the life she wanted and deserved. Cheers to you, Mom, for being the strong woman you are, someone I can write about in a book.

There are women I admire and women I learned a lot from, such as my grandmother. Let me share with you a little more about my grandmother's incredible story because it will give you an insight into why I do so much for divorcing and divorced women. You can always learn from any story; this one just so happens to have a ton of lessons stemming from not just one divorce but two.

My famous grandmother was very career oriented, and she worked on two television shows in the 1960's. Right after her first divorce, she held two jobs to support her family. She was a teacher during the day and a realtor at night and on the weekends. Her busy schedule meant that my mother and her brothers were alone most of the time. My grandmother did what she had to do to get by, including showing up with her poodle to an audition for a children's television show. She went on to become the host of that show (with her poodle as the co-host, of course.) The show was called *Claire and Coco* and ran for many years. Coco was my mother's childhood standard white poodle. The taxi drivers would fight over who had the privilege of bringing Coco home, and she even got her nails done for every show. I don't even get that many manicures in a year! The second show she hosted was a women's talk show, called *Women Talk*. She would have celebrities on such as Sonny and Cher. It is impressive and highly respectable for a woman to have had such a tremendous career in the 1960's.

Claire was a beautiful and extremely charming woman, who had a wicked sense of humor. She was witty with a very high IQ, and went to Cornell at the age of 17, for goodness sake, which explains why my mother is so smart.

The reason I'm telling you all about my grandmother is to explain that even someone as successful and intelligent as she was could get duped…and she was…by her ex-husband. Let me set the scene.

It all started when my grandmother got a call from the ER in Bethesda, Maryland, asking if her husband does this often. She asked what the nurse meant, and the nurse then explained that her husband had been dropped off in a pink nightgown sporting pink toenails and fingernails.

Now, that I have your attention, let's rewind a bit to show you the whole picture. My mother was four when her parents divorced, and she remembers being asked by the judge who she wanted to live with. Already, through that instance, we know how far we've come in the divorce process throughout the years, so hopefully, no children are asked this question in front of a judge and both of their parents anymore. Anyway, the judge decided my mother and her brothers would live with both parents during their childhood. Remember, my grandmother had a highly successful career, so my mother was raised more by nannies and housekeepers than by her own mother. Her life wasn't perfect. She was bipolar and back then they didn't know nearly as much as they do now. To manage her disorders, she would take diet pills during the week, which was basically speed back then, and sleeping pills on the weekend. Not the best mixture for someone who's bipolar. Unfortunately, my grandmother was never able to find happiness in her life. She would always say, "If I could just have a bigger house, more money, or more clothes, then I would be happy." Or my favorite quote of hers: "You can be miserable poor or miserable rich, and I'd rather be miserable rich!"

A few years after the divorce, my grandmother remarried a Washington, D.C. lawyer named Fred. They were living in Maryland at the time they started dating and then got married. My grandmother retired to the Outer Banks in North Carolina while Fred continued to work in D.C., and visit her only a few times a year. It seems as if they'd married one another for the money and financial security since they were both successful. They each had their own motives, I guess.

Fred was an alcoholic and told us he had been sober many times. It was always interesting to see his large glass of "water," oops, I mean vodka, beside him. He wasn't fooling any of us when he would say how thirsty he was for water. He loved to tell us he was going to Alcoholic Anonymous conventions throughout the year to speak; what a great guy, right? Even as a young girl, I knew something was off when he would fall flat on his face while playing catch on the beach. He'd even cheat when he'd play me and my brother in poker. He'd seriously cheat a 6 and 8-year-old at cards while knowing my father could see his antics the whole time. Even with his faults and her faults, too, the marriage seemed to work for them. They'd only see each other a few times a year, usually when the entire family had gathered. But, let's fast forward 34 years into their marriage to when my grandmother got the legendary call from the ER because of her husband's stroke.

My mother and grandmother found out that Fred was a cross-dressing, alcoholic lawyer in D.C., with two mistresses on the side that he was putting through college, and whose rents he was paying. He had also bought a Mercedes for each of them. One received a $5,000 Gucci bag! We were all extremely confused since he'd always been very cheap with us. A $5,000 bag! He probably would have spent $5 on my bag, not $5,000! Anyway, the one mistress is the one who left him at the hospital and the one who told my grandmother, "He is your problem now."

When my mother and grandmother went to his apartment during the time he was recovering from a stroke, they found his whole other life. Those alcoholic conventions were in fact, cross-dressing conventions, and boy did he have a fabulous wardrobe. I'm talking ball gowns, wigs, bags, accessories, and probably the most *horrifying* red leather bustier and matching skin-tight pants. I'm sorry, but a 350-pound man should not wear skin-tight red leather. Really, no one of any size should! Fred would dress up as a woman at the conventions, and his mistresses would dress as men. He spent a lot of money on his wardrobe and other life, but I guess that's the bonus of living hours away from your wife and having separate credit cards.

He was a sneaky and savvy lawyer, too. They also found out he had put my grandmother's two houses in his name, and he had even taken out a second mortgage on one house, so he could put the money toward his fabulous life. Needless to say, my grandmother immediately filed for a divorce. She also canceled their joint credit cards and took him off her bank accounts. Three attorneys fought for him in the divorce and spent a ridiculous amount of my grandmother's money.

My grandmother got her share back in the divorce including the houses and their equity, but the divorce put a drain on both her finances and emotions. There's a lot more to this story, such as Fred pushing my grandmother on a cruise ship and breaking her neck. And the fact that he then called my mother to say he was leaving Claire at a hospital in France. In the end, blood is thicker than water, but we won't get into all the nitty gritty now. The point of telling my grandmother's story is to provide background on why I am so passionate about helping people during a divorce and what we can learn from what happened to my grandmother.

Here are some points to be made from this tale:

1. Do not drag your children into your divorce battles, like my grandmother and grandfather did during the first divorce.

2. Always keep track of your credit cards and bank accounts.

3. Review the titles to your house, car, and any other personal property.

4. Once you know you are getting a divorce, get all your financial information together and organized, and then…

5. …please, do not marry a cross-dressing alcoholic with two mistresses!

Unfortunately, sometimes we have to learn lessons the hard way, especially when it comes to someone we love. So there; your family isn't the only crazy one out there! I think every family is a little nuts and the only normal family is really the abnormal one. Sadly, my grandfather's remarriage left the family in a bit of a circumstance as well.

During my grandparent's first divorce, the agreement stated my mother and her two brothers would live with both parents. This was a little difficult since my grandmother lived in Maryland and my grandfather lived in New York, but they made it happen. My mother would typically spend summers in New York with her father and his parents, which she loved to do. Not long after his divorce, he remarried a successful physical therapist, who was about 15 years younger. Now, my grandfather was way past the point of wanting more children, but for his new wife he made an exception, and they ended up having a daughter together.

Another part of the divorce agreement was for my grandfather to pay for my mother's college. Unfortunately, life happens and tragedy struck my mother during her sophomore year in college.

My mother was so excited her brothers were coming up to visit her and meet her new boyfriend, A. K. A. my father. But their visit wasn't about pleasantries. They made the trip to tell her in person her father had passed away from a heart attack. So, my mother and her brothers were dealing with the loss of their father, only to find out he didn't have a will in place. Not a good thing with a second marriage and a half sibling.

All my grandfather's possessions went to his wife, who refused to help pay for my mother's college. When I say, everything went to her stepmother, I mean my mother's grandmother's house, her father's antique sword and gun collection, and so many other things you can't replace. My mother worked through college, took out some student loans, and graduated all on her own.

My mother tried to stay close with her stepmom and half-sister throughout the years, but it wasn't easy since they would always remind her of what was theirs. Even when my grandmother passed away, her half-sister told my mother that part of the estate belonged to her. How on earth would the estate belong to her when she hadn't even been around when they'd gotten divorced? This put a strain on their relationship, and when her stepmom passed away, my mother never even knew because no one told her. Her half-sister was probably scared my mother would expect some inheritance, which wasn't the case at all.

There are some very important and crucial lessons to learn from her father's remarriage and here is my checklist of items:

1. Always have your estate documents in order, especially after your divorce. You want to make sure what you want to happen with your estate actually happens. The only way to do this is to meet with an attorney and draft your wills.

2. Update your power of attorney and living wills after a divorce since you probably named your ex-spouse as your power of attorney and healthcare proxy. You may not want them to make an important decision on your life after a divorce.

3. If need be, buy some life insurance to make sure there is money to send your children to college if you are no longer here. Life insurance exists to help your family stay in their house or protect them from going into debt if you pass away. The death benefit can help them live the life you probably want them to keep living.

4. Properly title your family heirlooms, such as your house, so they stay in the family like my great-grandmother's house.

I feel like I am an open book now that you know my family's dirty secrets. If my grandmother and mother can move on with their lives and not let the past dictate their future, you can, too. And I will be right next to you every step of the way. I have spoken with hundreds of women for my blog and through doing research for my book, and it is incredible to see how strong and resilient women can be. Sometimes we don't even know we can bounce back until we are pushed to the limits. A lot of the women I've interacted with kept pushing themselves forward for their children. We will do anything for our children and our family; it is our "mama bear" coming out, as I call it. Don't mess with my little dachshund or mama bear is coming!

Your first step in this journey is to decide who you are doing it for. Is it for your children, so they can see an amazing role model in their mom? For your spouse, so they will know you are a strong and independent woman? For your parents or loved ones? Or maybe you are doing it for yourself.

Take some time to think about it, write it down here.

I am transforming my life for:

_____

Remember who you are taking this adventure for because it will keep you motivated, grounded, and help to push you through the storm clouds.

One woman, whose husband had left 35 years ago and never looked back, did it for her daughters. Not only did he leave her, but he left them, too. He found another woman with children and basically adopted that family while leaving his own family completely. This woman had to start working with two daughters in school and her youngest who was only a baby. Luckily, her parents watched her baby while she went back to work as a teacher. When she was exhausted from working all day and taking courses at night, she would remember her girls. They were what helped her through the dark times, so she and her family could create their new happy memories. I could tell she was smiling when she talked about their new Friday night tradition: Girls Night Out. They'd go out for dinner, shopping, or take in a new movie. She had created a new and amazing life for her family, but it didn't happen overnight, and it wasn't easy. Her motivation for transforming was her daughters, and it is what got her through the tough times. It was all worth it to have all three daughters become very successful, bright, and beautiful young women.

Another woman did it in part for herself and in part for her parents. She'd needed financial support from her parents throughout her life and was sick of feeling dependent on them. They wanted to retire, and she knew something needed to change so they wouldn't feel burdened by her. Parents will always help their children even if it means jeopardizing their own lives. Even with the money they'd given her, she found herself in debt each month. Her spending and saving habits were crippling her, and the added financial support didn't change that.

She despised going to the grocery store. She was terrified if she used her debit card it would get declined, but she was even more afraid of using that card and going further into debt. She felt like she was failing herself, her parents, and her daughters. She lived this way for about 15 years when she decided it was finally time to make a change. During our first call, she explained she was screwed if she continued down the same path. It was a simple answer but straight to the point; she was screwed and knew it.

So, she took a stance and said, "Enough is enough. I can be financially independent." It didn't happen overnight, and at first, she had to borrow my belief that she could do it. Now, after a lot of hard work, getting herself out of debt, and not getting *back into* debt, she's realized her parents' help wasn't the solution. Her parents' money couldn't get her out of debt because she would find herself back in debt very quickly. More money wasn't changing the way she lived; more money wasn't changing her money beliefs and behaviors. She first thought her purpose for change was her parents, but as we went through her transformation, she learned it was for herself, too.

The last example I will share is a woman who did it for her ex-husband. Maybe it wasn't directly for her ex-husband, but she refocused her money goals more so she could get away from him. She was sick of feeling so dependent on his alimony and his money. What if he brought her back to trial to lower it? This thought hung over her head all day and night. She knew it would be a waste of her hard-earned money to pay for a lawyer to fight him; he liked to fight dirty. She had been working part-time and was trying to get more work since her children had gotten older. She felt stuck and didn't know she had so many options. So, she decided to make a change to retake her life and finances. She wants to feel confident with her money and not trapped by him anymore, and this is what drives her every day within her transformation.

These are just a few examples of what is driving the women around us to change. What is your motive? Why did you pick up this book? What made you turn the page? Take some time to dive in deep to learn your reason for transformation. I'd love to hear your reason, so please share it by emailing https://www.jessicaweaver.com/contact.

or post it on my Jessica Weaver, Wealth Advisor Facebook page. Sharing your reason will encourage other women who feel trapped and stuck to convert their lives, too.

Remember what the reason was to alter my life? In the beginning, it was for my happiness and to make my father proud, proud to have his daughter who loved working with him and who loved following in his footsteps. I wanted so badly for it to work that I couldn't imagine doing anything else for a career. And this is what propelled me forward, but it became so much bigger than just me. The more lives I've helped to change, the more enjoyment and happiness I find in my work. So, it isn't about my happiness or earning more money. It's about the women I work with, and the knowledge that no other advisor will strive to work as hard or give as much potential value as I will. And it is the fact that these women could be worse off if they work with someone else because no one will care as much as I do.

Chapter 3: Your Relationship with Money May Be Jeopardizing Your Future

"If I ever let my head down it will be to admire my shoes."
~Unknown

We all have our money stories, stories we grew up around, stories we've created for ourselves, and stories others have imposed on us. These money stories are what shape our lives. If you grew up in a household where you used every coupon, budgeted every penny, and never splurged, that is your money story. What you do with the money story is up to you. You can use it and live by it; you can rebel against it, or you can just let it be a story. Your money stories are NOT written in stone. They are just stories. Some stories we remember forever and some we forget immediately. We get to **decide** if they shape the rest of our lives or not.

Let me ask you, what are your current money stories? Let's start with what you grew up around because we either embrace those stories or we protest them. Some people who grew up in a family on a tight budget stay frugal their entire lives while others become a bit of a spendthrift. If you grew up with debt your whole life, then debt might be the only story you know how to live by. We need to identify our stories and see if they are helping our lives or jeopardizing them.

One woman grew up in a wealthy family and was quite accustomed to getting whatever she needed and wanted. When she got married, the trend continued even though her income and her husband's income wasn't near what she grew up around. It didn't matter; she still wanted luxury vacations, a million-dollar house, and fancy cars. It was the only way she knew how to live, even though it was causing friction with her husband and added stress about their financial future. If debt becomes the only way to keep up with a certain lifestyle, then is it really the best thing for your family?

Another person I know grew up in a lower-income family, where they needed to coupon and budget. She was so sick of being tied down by money, she rebelled and got herself into credit card debt pretty quickly after college. The stress from the mounting debt outweighed the pros of a nice wardrobe, but it took her some time and guidance to realize it. Are your money stories adding stress to your life? In today's world, we don't need any extra stress in our lives. Let's take care of the money and financial stress now, so you have one less **MAJOR** item to worry over. Sound good to you?

I've noticed a growing issue facing people after college, and the similar money stories they all graduate with as well. It seems more and more of the graduates are getting financial support from their parents. I think the last survey I read said about 50 percent of people in their twenties are receiving some sort of help. According to an article on *Money Talks News*[2], 68 percent of college students expect their parents to support them after graduation, and 65 percent of parents plan on supporting them.

My theory is that the graduates are so used to living their certain lifestyle that it took their parents 30 plus years of working hard to obtain. Yet, they want the lifestyle immediately. The nice apartment, house, luxury car, designer wardrobe, fancy nails, etc.

---

[2]*Krystal Steinmetz, "Most Students Expect Parents' Financial Help After College," http://www. moneytalksnews. com/most-students-expect-parents-financial-support-after-college/, (May 20, 2015).*

The list goes on and on, but the bottom line is that they expect to have all these perks on a small, starter salary. It's not going to happen overnight, not without some support.

So, before you notice the $1,000 handbag on a 20-something, think about who paid for it. At least, that's what I do!

Now, we've taken care of the money stories from our childhood, but what about those from our adult life? Or maybe from a significant other who had a different story than yours, so you adopted theirs. Is your adult story: money will always stress me out? I will never be in control over my money? I will never have enough money? I will always have debt? Remember, these are just stories we say to ourselves; they don't have to be our rules. They are **NOT** permanent. They can be adjusted, modified, or completely thrown out the window if need be.

Does your spouse always spend ruthlessly? Have you adopted this story, too, let it cause tension in your marriage, or addressed it? It is very difficult for two people to have the same view on money, how much to make, spend, and save. But, it's what keeps the world interesting, right? It is also the reason why so many marriages end...because of money issues. Knowing what our stories are and sharing them, can help your spouse understand why you are the way you are with money and why they are the way they are. Usually, when you can't agree, it means you will remain in the exact situation you've been in for the past year, 5 years, or 30 years.

To help clear up why you are the way you are with moneexplore your stories. I want you to write down your top five money stories. These are the stories you live by, grew up with, and the stories you fall back on.

1._____

2._____

3._____

4._____

5._____

Now you know why you've been living the way you have with your money or at least have a clearer picture. How have these stories impacted your life so far? Let's take some time to explore the impacts of our money beliefs and see if you are stuck in your life because of them.

Being stuck in your life is costing you more than you think. It is paralyzing your life today and jeopardizing your future as well. Trust me; I know from experience when I was unhappy at work. I sat at my desk all day thinking *someday, I will love what I do*. Someday, but not today, right? How many times do you think *maybe one day I'll have enough to go on that trip to Europe? Maybe in retirement, I'll finally be able to take care of my health? Maybe if I win the lottery, I'll be able to help my family?* Someday, but **NOT** today. Are you sick of it being someday and not today? I was so sick of it when I, at last, took action to change my future because, in the end, you have to ask yourself *why are we waiting to live the lives we want? Why are we giving up today?* Is it because we think there is no way possible we can do it now? In the end, why not now?

It all comes down to living your self-worth. When you are "stuck" or "trapped" in your current life, it means you are accepting that you are not living up to your self-worth. Have you thought about how much it costs you to be "stuck" at your current job? What about being in a bad relationship for

1 year, 5 years, or even 20 years too long; what is that costing you? And another big one: how much is that downward debt spiral really taking from you and your family? Since we can't measure the effects of these implications on our lives, we don't really think about them. But they are all there, and they are all costing us the most precious thing around: **ourselves**.

I want you to think about all the ways being stuck is affecting your life. What are the emotions surrounding it? How much energy is it draining from you each day and how many years have you been affected? What are the snowball effects of impacting your family and friends, because trust me, they see it and feel it, too. You might not feel like yourself at times, and as a result, you might act out toward the people you love. I've done it, and I've seen it happen.

When your friend is stressed, exhausted, and overworked, she probably isn't her bubbly usual self. If you ask my husband, he'll say right away how different I am when I'm stressed or frustrated. And it affects our relationship. A few mothers I've spoken with admit to fighting more with their children when they are concerned about money. Some don't sleep, and so when their children whine, after only two hours of sleep, mom's reaction is probably to send an outburst right back at them. Others get in fights with their spouses over where the money is coming from to pay all the bills, especially the one for "the brand new flat screen TV you said wasn't in the budget." Then spouses go to bed angry and the date night that used to be fun and sexy turns to arguing about money again. Most likely, without the makeup sex. I don't think money fights usually end with makeup sex. Let me know if I'm wrong. I'd have to rethink my husband's and my fights.

Our unhappiness with our lives touches those around us. If it didn't, I don't think my mother would pray every night for me to eventually calm down with work. I must be lashing out at her, too. Sorry, mom!

Write down all the things, people, concerns, and fears you want to discard from your life. Some popular ones are social media, negative people, money stress, fighting with your spouse or ex-spouse, etc.

_____

_____

_____

_____

I do this exact exercise during each of my Discovery Calls and at the end of my events. Some people can't stop writing while others take a while to really get started. When you are writing, feel the weight being lifted from your body. Each time you put pen to paper, imagine your concerns drifting away from you in a negativity bubble, as I like to call it. Say to yourself, as each item on your list moves farther away from you, "I don't need this negativity/concern/fear in my life." As it evaporates into the sky, let all the emotions, energy, and negativity follow it. You are freeing yourself of those feelings you no longer want. How do you feel now? Remember this state of relaxation, happiness, or whatever your sensation is because it will help keep those negative thoughts at bay.

It is time to decide if we will continue down this path until our life is over, or if we will say, "Enough is enough! My life is worth living!" I have chosen the latter as you know because I am meant to transform women's lives, and I hope I can transform your life, too. Now that you've thought about all that you'd like to shred from your life and all the energy and emotions that go along with it, think about all that you want. Write down what you want for your life, and don't limit yourself either:

_____

_____

_____

_____

Think about what your life can be, and how it will affect those around you. Do you think they will notice the change and want to change, too? At first, people might be nervous or apprehensive about your new direction in life. And that is fine. They want to keep you safe and comfortable, and what is safe is continuing your current patterns and life. (Even if it is hurting you. And they do this since no one likes change). Change is scary; change is new; it's different from what we know. Well, obviously; but change is also the only way to escape being stuck and unhappy. Change is a must, and life is built on decisions. As they say, "The only constant is change," so should we try hiding from it or embrace it? You got it, embrace it!! How will you feel once you get there? Is this feeling worth the change? It is time to start living the life you want, just like my favorite quote advises: "Ten years from now, make sure you can say you chose your life, you didn't settle for it." ~*Mandy Hale*

I had a Discovery Call with a woman who was newly divorced, and I asked her to share with me what she wants for her new life. I even had her fill out a form asking the same question, and both times she could barely tell me. I had to get her into the right mindset since her whole life she had been in debt, and then in a bad marriage, and she'd had very little self-worth. These were her money stories, and what she was living by, so she didn't know there could be other ways to live. After coaching her through the exercise, I couldn't stop her from rattling off more things she wanted for her new life. It was awesome to hear: no more debt, traveling, buying a house, getting her son through college; she wanted to be independent with her money, to save for retirement, to work less and get paid more, and it went on and on.

Like I said, it wasn't easy for her, and she had a tough time opening her eyes to her current financial situation. It can be scary and overwhelming to look at our money, right? There are times when even I don't want to look at my credit card bill, but we need to in order to move forward. If we don't know where we are currently, there is no way we can get to where we want to be. If we don't weigh ourselves before stepping on the scale, three months later, how will we know how much weight we've lost? So, embrace where you are today, and I am going to challenge you to be thankful for where you are right in this moment. Even if you are only thankful you are reading this book, say it out loud. I am thankful! I am grateful because I know where I am and where I want to be! This the first step toward getting to your goals.

No matter how much farther you want to be; you've still worked so hard to get here. I'm sure you're like me, and you've had setbacks along the way. Those setbacks can be so frustrating and exhausting, and I'm sure there are times when you want to just stop. You might be about to break through to the next level when something happens, and suddenly you feel all the ground you've covered, is lost. I felt this same way when I had to bring my dog, Duke, to the vet late one night. We had another scare with his back, and if you don't know the story, here is Duke's history.

In August of last year, my husband, Duke, and I were at my parent's house when Duke herniated a disc in his back. He is a dachshund, and the breed has a bad history with degenerative disc disease. He instantly became paralyzed in the back half of his small body, and by small, I mean 8 pounds (10 pounds, if my father watches him for a week.) It was such a scary moment when he started dragging himself away because he was in so much pain and had no idea what to do. I always thought I'd be calm and collected when such an occurrence arose, but I was so wrong. My husband had to snap me out of my tears and shock.

Luckily there were four of us, so we could rush him to the animal hospital close by. My father was on the iPad calling us with directions, my husband driving like a madman, my mom reporting the directions to us, and I'm holding poor Duke trying to calm him down. They rushed surgery on his back, and after a call with the doctor at 1 AM, informed us the surgery had gone well. They'd removed so much fluid around his disc that they said they'd never seen anything like it before. After a few days, Duke gained some feeling back in his legs, and after a week, he started to gain some movement as well. These were all very good signs for a full recovery.

My husband and I were so committed to getting Duke back to the all-star self he had been that we researched nonstop how to help him. We started him in physical therapy twice a week and then once a week on an underwater treadmill. He also goes to a chiropractor once a month to make sure everything is properly aligned. He does rehab exercises twice a day for rewards, which are his meals, and we have him walking about a half a mile a day. Duke is doing great, although sometimes he does walk like a drunk pirate or a penguin. He also isn't allowed to do stairs, or jump or climb up or down on anything. But even after doing all these preventative measures, his back still acted up. One night, my husband went to feed him, and when he touched his back, Duke yelped and lost control of his bladder. We rushed him to the vet, and they thought he'd aggravated the same spot in his back because it was badly inflamed. So, Duke went on crate rest for three weeks, with painkillers, anti-inflammatory meds, and muscle relaxers. No walks, exercises, or play time, which is very hard for a 3-year-old dachshund.

As upset as we were with poor Duke's injury, I started thinking how much worse it would have been if we hadn't done all we'd done. If we hadn't gotten his muscles strong again and got him walking properly. I am so thankful it was only aggravated and that he was not on his way to another herniated disc. Eric and I kept 3 different 24/7 animal hospitals on our phone for months just in case it happened again. Duke spent 3 weeks on crate rest or the best we could do with his crate rest (his sad eyes are very hard to deny.) He is doing much better now and is back to his daily walks and exercises. From this experience, we learned not to push him too hard since he can't tell us when his back hurts or is sore. It would be so much easier if he could talk! Anyway, we learned some new things about his condition, and are thankful for the support we have around him. We can't express how grateful we are that our instincts were to get Duke strong and walking again. Who knows where he would be if we hadn't listened to our gut feelings.

So, I'm challenging you to look at whatever setback you've had recently and to think how much further back you'd be if you hadn't put in all that hard work and all those long hours. Maybe your 401(k) isn't as big as you'd hoped it would be, but at least you have a 401(k), and you have a goal for it. More importantly, you're aware of your 401(k), which is the first step to getting it back on track. Or maybe you've returned to the dating scene after your divorce, and haven't had much luck. But at least you are out there trying, which is such a huge step and not a relaxing one in the least. Wherever you are in your life, be proud of it. It took a lot to get here.

I see this more and more with the women I work with after their divorce is over. They might not be in the best possible financial situation or where they thought they'd be at this age, but thank goodness, they aren't where they were a year ago. The only way they can move forward is addressing their situation now, being thankful for where they are, and to start putting their plan together. It is very easy to have hindsight bias and say to yourself *woulda, shoulda, coulda.* But we can't go back and change our lives, can we? So, why waste all that energy and negativity thinking *if only I'd done this, I would be where I want to be.*

A particular woman who came to me for help did just that; she kept repeating to herself, *well if I only I'd divorced him two years ago.* Maybe she should have, but we will never know since she didn't. She kept going in circles because any progress we made with her PRESENT situation was paused when she backtracked to thinking about what if she had divorced him two years ago. She probably wasn't in the right state of mind to get divorced two years ago. There are always outside factors affecting us and our decisions or ability to make a rational decision. In her situation, her husband left his stable and successful career to focus on a project. She was a homemaker, who had to go back to work to pay the high mortgage and all their other expenses. Her new salary wasn't cutting it, so instead of building up more debt, they sold the house. This had occurred two years ago, but she was still in shock over the huge change their life had taken. Sometimes, there is only so much change we can mentally take, and it is only once it sinks in that we can move forward.

Compare it to when a person loses 50 pounds; they need their body and mind to adjust to their new body. Metabolism is different, they need new clothes, and people will most likely see the change before the person can even wrap their head around it. Or when celebrities go from making nothing each week to millions of dollars. They tend to overspend and live too extravagantly, thinking the money will always come in. They don't have time to catch up to the money and fame, and unfortunately, so many crash and burn. They wind up broke, in debt, and fighting their way back on *Dancing with the Stars*.

It took the woman I work with two years to process the change in her life, but she might stay stuck if she can't move past her hindsight bias. So, even if you are having trouble like she is, decide to take one step forward. Your step can be a tiptoe, but it should be something to keep yourself moving in the right direction. For her, it was a call with me where we made huge progress to get her over the hurdle. Now we are doing a strategy session to see how we can move her even further toward her goals and where she wants to be, to start creating her plan, so she won't spend the next 10 years thinking, *what if?*

There will be times when you fall back into your old habits, which for my client, means being stuck in the past. The key is to identify these old habits and when you are prone to your old bad habits. But what kind of habits are we talking about? The ones that will keep you stuck in your life, backtracking or that will prevent you from obtaining your goals. For me, it was shopping and overspending when I was tired, stressed, and frustrated with work. I'd go to the mall on my way home and spend more than I normally would have. When we are emotional or exhausted or both, we tend to make a rash or bad decision. We just aren't thinking clearly like our normal, level-headed self. At least, level-headed for the most part!

These are called your spending triggers or as I call them, your "bad decision triggers." It is why we need to know what our triggers are, so then we can decide whether to wait to make a big decision when we are in a better state of mind.

Here is a list of possible triggers. It would be extremely beneficial to you if you circled your triggers:

- Tired

- Shame

- Anger

- Confused

- Lost

- Frustrated

- Sad

- Stressed

- Overworked

- Overwhelmed

- Write your own:_____

First, what are your triggers? Second, what happens when these triggers go off? Do you shop too much like I do? Maybe indulge in a chocolate cake or a bag of potato chips? Do you react differently to your ex-spouse when he misses a pick-up with your children? One great piece of advice from a divorced woman was to never let her emotions affect the relationship between her ex-husband and her daughter. If she did let that happen, their relationship would be even more strained, if not, nonexistent. While you might feel great in the moment telling your ex to take a hike, you aren't doing your own life or children any good.

Usually, when we make a rash decision, we feel awesome and justified, but it doesn't last. It is a fleeting emotion and a fleeting satisfaction, which leaves us feeling even worse afterward. When I get home from the mall to see my credit card balance, my retail therapy quickly turns into buyer's remorse. So, instead of acting on an intense emotion, take time to process the real impacts of your decision, not just on you but on your family. I have a 4-step process to help fix our rash decision making:

1. First, we must admit we have a problem... I am Jessica, and I have a shopping problem.

2. Write down the times or days when you spend money.

3. Think about your emotions during those times.

4. What can we replace your bad habit with?

    a. The replacement should be small and achievable.

    b. Make it something positive, and

    c. Have it address what you are trying to avoid, such as stress, which you hope to de-stress.

The best part is that the replacement can be a reward for yourself. And what is great about rewards is that they keep us on track and motivated. If your boss pushes your stress level to a new high, what can you do to de-stress? Maybe you can try meditation, massage your temples, get a back rub, manicure, or go for a walk. Or, all of the above, if the boss is that bad! One woman even suggested wearing a heart rate monitor to see who in your office raises your heart rate the most. It can also be effective to use throughout the day to pinpoint when you are frazzled or relaxed.

Just so you know, I take my own advice and instead of shopping at the mall on my way home, I will bring my dog for a walk. Simply from making this small change, I have more energy, my husband is happy, and we can save more money for our goals. Now I will ask you, what will your replacement or replacements be?

Remember, it usually isn't all mimosas and butterflies when you are going through a new life transition, and sometimes you might feel completely blind and alone. If it were so easy, we'd all be rich, happy, and where we want to be. Instead, you'll have setbacks and side steps, and everything in between. But it is during those tough times when you find your strength to break through and keep going. So, be thankful for how far you've come, and appreciate where you are right now. Even if you have miles more to go, think of how many miles you've already conquered. I do the same thing, literally, when I run. If I have five miles more to go, I try to remember I've already run four miles. As Joyce Meyer said, "I'm not where I need to be, but thank God, I'm not where I used to be." Amen to that, sister!

With your mind focused on gratitude for your life, we can allow ourselves to stop living in the past and move toward our future. It takes too much energy to hold on to bad emotions, and it keeps us stuck. We have to let go of all that is getting in our way, our old money stories, our old money habits, and our old emotions.

"You have to stop thinking you'll be stuck forever.

We feel like our heart will never heal or

We'll never get out of this impossible struggle.

Don't confuse a season for a lifetime.

Even your trials have an expiration date.

You will grow, life will change, things will work out."
~Brittany Moses

Now we are ready for change and can embrace the hard work ahead of us because we are worth it in the end, aren't we? Isn't it worth it to invest some time, money, and energy into your life to elevate it? If you don't agree, you can borrow my belief that your life is worth it.

We have a much better idea of why we are where we are with our money, we know what we want to discard from our life, and we have identified what we want. Your next step is to start working toward your new life. And it is now time to create your new life and your new money mantra. Your money mantra will become your real-life money story and your new belief around money.

Maybe your old money mantra was "I will always be in debt," and you probably have *always* been in debt. Your new mantra is "I will live debt-free. I will have an abundant amount of money." Or, if your old mantra was "I will never understand finances," your new one is "I will be in total control over my finances."

Your turn: what was your old mantra?

What is your new money mantra?

How will your new money mantra work for you? How will it catapult you into living the life you deserve? During the tough times when you feel yourself being pulled backward, remember your new mantra. If you're having a bad day, remember why you are doing all your hard work and repeat your mantra to keep yourself present and grounded.

I guess my old mantra was "Success is defined by how many designer brands you can wear at once." I know, very shallow, and I hate admitting it. The root of my old mantra started when I went to private high school where a Coach backpack was the standard backpack. So, my good old JanSport backpack didn't quite cut it and forget about when kids started driving. It was all Mercedes, BMWs, and Audis in the parking lot. And these were teenagers' first cars! I could tell their parents were successful, so, unfortunately, the luxury brands and high-end labels were my first impression of the definition of success. Luckily, I now know the truth and how success is different for everyone. The more women I help, the more successful I feel, and therefore, my new money mantra is "The more women I help, the more happiness and success I will have."

We don't have to define our lives by our past money stories. We can rewrite our stories by creating a new money mantra to live by. And please don't get swept up by the keeping up with the Joneses syndrome. It is very similar to my old mantra where we define ourselves by the "stuff" we have. It is always a losing game to play because someone will *always* have a nicer car, nicer house, and nicer "stuff." Dig deep into what your new mantra will be because it will be your new code of conduct for your life.

49

If you can't think of one, here is a list you can try on for size:

- I will have a plentiful retirement.

- I will be in total control over my money.

- I will be confident with my money decisions.

- I will not be a slave to money; it will only be a tool to get the life I want.

- I love paying the bills; they allow me to live my life.

The last one reminds me of a woman who hated paying her bills. She would set about five alarms to remind her to pay the bills each month, and it's not like she didn't know it was the end of the month and time to pay those darn bills. She knew they were coming, and yet, even with the alarms going off, she was still late every month. She would pay late fees among late fees and hated herself every time she paid them. I explained that while she hated paying the bills, she couldn't wish them away. So, we dug deeper into why her money mantra was "I hate paying the bills." It wasn't just the mere act of sending the checks out every month. It was more than that. In the end, she was terrified of not having enough money to cover the bills every month. And it was mostly on her to manage the finances, keep track of their spending, and to make sure they had enough money each month. It caused her stress, frustration, and affected her health since she had trouble sleeping. She gained weight since she was too tired after work to go to the gym. She fought more with her children and husband. After speaking, it finally hit her how many other areas of her life were being affected by those darn bills. We put a plan together to get her on her way to fix the monthly bill issues, but in order to do so, we had to create a new way to pay the bills and to share the responsibilities of their family's money.

About 90 percent of the women I've interviewed for this book have had a money mantra of "I'm making one bad financial decision after another." Or, "I never know whether I'm making a good decision for myself and my family." When we don't know the impacts of our choices, they can become so overwhelming and daunting that we don't do anything. We remain frozen because a confused mind does nothing, and an overwhelmed mind does nothing. So, guess what they did? NOTHING! Now, their new mantras are "I will be in total control over my money," and "I will be confident and secure with my money choices." It's amazing what a little switch in our beliefs and thinking will do. We begin to believe our new mantras as they become a part of our daily lives. We see some success with them, which only fuels more beliefs into them and ourselves. We can transform our lives to match how we value ourselves and to get what we want and deserve.

Our new money mantras will start moving us in the right direction. How, you might ask? Because when we start thinking a certain way, our behaviors start aligning with those beliefs and values. It's astounding what a little belief followed by some action can do for our lives. One belief, one step forward can make a dramatic impact. Bigger than you probably thought at first, or what you won't believe until you see it for yourself. One small change leads to more and more until we are living a different life than we were a year ago.

I'm living proof of it, where I was two years ago is *nothing* compared to where I am today. The next step is exactly that, a step forward. Now, it's time to take action.

Your call to action for Chapter 3 is to:

Write 3 things you are thankful for in your life:

1._____

2._____

3._____

Write 3 things you want to discard from your life:

1._____

2._____

3._____

Write 3 things you want to add to your life:

1._____

2._____

3._____

Chapter 4: Becoming an Action Taker

"A strong woman looks a challenge in the eye and gives it a wink." ~Gina Carey

I was helping my best friend pack up her closet after seven years of adding clothes to it without eliminating any. Obviously, it took us a few hours, but she went above and beyond our expectations of how many articles of clothing she got rid of. I was really impressed. There were at least 17 pairs of jeans, for goodness sake, that now have new owners. There were old bridesmaid dresses from lifetime's ago, old work clothes she hasn't worn in years, and her old wedding dress. What to do with a wedding dress once you get divorced?

Along with the other clothes she's donating, her wedding dress is being given to a great organization. The organization gives dresses new lives for women, who don't have the means to buy their own wedding dress. If you have something similar in your closet, think of it this way, you will be able to bring someone else happiness through giving something that brought you happiness years ago. When you reframe your thoughts, it changes your feelings about releasing something very emotional and close to your heart, and that probably even brings you bad memories. More importantly, it allows you to move on, and in my friend's case, into the arms of a wonderful man. I don't think he would like the wedding dress moving in with her other stuff.

We went on purging and packing for a few hours, and while we did, reminisced a bit. You know how girlfriends do, the past, present, and dreams for the future. She was over-the-moon excited for the next chapter of her life, moving in with a man she finally feels is her best friend and a true partner in life. Someone who likes adventure as much as she does, who brings her flowers out of the blue, though it seems to happen most of the time, and most importantly, who loves her as much as she loves him. Someone who loves to cook her dinner, and yells at her if she tries to do the dishes. Now, what you don't know is that my friend already thought she was in love and had found her partner in life.

She met her ex-husband in college, and they dated for about seven years before they got married. They were married for about five years but separated for a year in the middle. The problems that caused the separation never were fixed, so when they got back together, they continued in the same manner for a few more years. Then he said those four dreaded words..."I want a divorce." I could see her life spinning while she tried to fight for her happiness again. In the end, she knew the divorce was best for her. And the farther she got from the divorce, the more she found her old self. Then she found love again, but this time, a deeper love and a love that is reciprocal.

So, when she was standing in her closet going through the twentieth pair of jeans, it wasn't a surprise when she said she was so happy and thankful he had asked for the divorce. Because if he hadn't, she wouldn't be where she is today. She would be stuck in a bad relationship and "kind of" happy. She'd still be in a one-way relationship where she felt so alone even with him lying next to her in bed at night. She wouldn't be moving in with an amazing guy, who just took her on a fabulous island vacation. She would have been **stuck**.

The point of sharing my friend's story with you is to impart that sometimes we need to take action with our lives, and still there are other times when we are forced into a new chapter. If you are stuck in your life, you have the undeniable ability to take a stance and take action. My friend could have gotten back with her ex; he's asked her multiple times, but she knew it wouldn't solve anything. She would have stayed stuck, and she is too strong for that. You might need to tiptoe right now, maybe just set time aside each week to think about your next move, but you need to start moving in a direction that makes you happy again and to elevate your life. Our lives are too short to stay rooted in one place, and your life will zip right past you if you remain where you are today.

A great book about moving toward your happiness is *The Lighthouse Method: How Busy Overloaded Moms Can Get Unstuck and Figure Out What to Do with Their Lives* by Stacy Kim.

In the book, Stacy explains why women tend to get stuck in their day-to-day lives. It starts with the concept that women are selfless givers. We always want to take care of everyone else before we take care of ourselves. But if we give all our attention and energy to everyone else, we will never have enough time to think about what we want. This describes how my friend was with her ex-husband; she put everything into taking care of him and his needs. Problem was, he didn't do the same.

Women also tend to be perfectionists. Sounds about right! We want to plan for everything and will only act when we feel we are fully capable and knowledgeable about our choices. If we aren't confident, then we won't go out on the limb and try something new or apply for that promotion. What happens if you plan every detail out, but nothing goes according to plan? Good question, and as Stacy says, "You can plan all you want, but what matters most is taking your first **step**."

She calls these little steps rowing, as in you are rowing in your boat toward a lighthouse or your goal. And the critical point she makes about the "rowing" is to ensure it is enjoyable. Hard work doesn't have to be grueling and exhausting. If you find yourself dragging your stilettos in the ground then maybe it is time to "row" somewhere else or to identify a new goal.

Stacy recommends finding something every day to bring you happiness. I personally love the idea, especially in a world where we are always on the go. You can easily end the day, without having done one thing for yourself or for your enjoyment. I always take my dog for a walk either in the morning or in the evening or sometimes both, and it is probably the one thing I love doing every time I do it. I didn't realize how much a simple walk with my little dachshund, Duke, brightens my mood after a long day at the office. It helps me digest what happened during work before I have to tackle my house chores and cook dinner.

Stacy and I touched base about her book, and she gave me some advice for anyone who seems to be floundering for an extended period of time. Maybe you have a goal of going back to work after leaving to raise your children or to take care of your parents. Or, maybe you are newly-divorced and are trying to build a new life, but seem to be getting nowhere. You just can't seem to find the right first steps to get your feet wet. She explained if you are struggling to find your lighthouse or have been rowing for too long, then you are probably being pulled in too many directions. You might be switching paths too often or not taking the "most enjoyable direction." She states it is hard for women to give themselves full permission to go after what they really want. One way to conquer this is to give yourself a time limit, such as two to three months. If after the two or three months, you aren't happy, then it is time to change the route to your lighthouse. The key is to give it all your attention for those months. You have my permission to put the focus back on yourself, to be vulnerable, and to allow yourself to make a mistake. But remember, have fun!

We can plan all we want, but there will always be new obstacles we have to face that weren't in our blueprint. Just start rowing your boat toward your lighthouse, and you'll find your way. And in this chapter, you'll learn how to start taking action and what happens after you've begun to find your rhythm. Women have a tremendous life rhythm. We just have to find yours again.

All it takes is a decision for you to choose to value your life and take a step toward it. It's never just *if I had more money, if I could just get out of debt*, or *if I just had a bigger house*. It isn't, right? Because if it were, we would be doing it. It's to have financial security, to be confident in our choices, and to be in control of our money. Money affects every aspect of our life. It can open doors or shut doors for us, too.

Here is my 4-step guide to taking action TODAY, not tomorrow:

1. Make a decision to change.

2. Gain clarity over your new direction in life.

3. Implement and be accountable.

4. Repeat steps 1 through 3.

Let's dig deeper into the four steps:

1. Make a decision to change; decide your life is worth the change and hard work.

Procrastinating usually comes up around now, but don't let it happen to you. Procrastination is the enemy to wealth, and it is the enemy to getting what you want. We can all procrastinate and lounge on our comfy couch in our pajamas, and it can continue in this way for another 10 years or so. However, in 10 years, you'll wake up in the same exact situation to find you've just wasted another decade of your life. I know we all love to procrastinate especially when the things we are avoiding make us uncomfortable and anxious. Usually, money and finances make us uncomfortable, anxious, oh, and STRESSED. But avoiding our money doesn't make it go away. Ignoring your pile of debt doesn't mean someone magically will pay it off. Ignoring your investment accounts doesn't mean they will automatically grow in the right direction.

Think of it another way. Let's say you have a wedding coming up, and you **need** to find a bombshell dress. One where the instant you put it on, you feel freaking fabulous. I know you know what I'm talking about. Hugs all the right curves, maybe forgiving in some other areas, and your date can't stop staring at your butt. But before you find the dress, you commit yourself to losing a few pounds. So, you wait a few months to start looking, then a few months turns into a year, and still no dress. Finally, it is the night before the wedding, and you find yourself in a dead sweat in the dressing room with dozens of dresses but no contenders. Let me ask you, did procrastinating benefit you or endanger your chances of finding THAT dress? You'll be showing up to the wedding in an old dress that probably has a stain on your back, maybe a hole under your armpit, and you'll hope no one notices. If this is the case **just** for a dress, imagine how procrastinating with your life and money can turn out for you.

But since you are already on Chapter 4, I'm guessing you've decided it is time to change and NOT procrastinate. Just in case, you decide to delay along the way, remember the dress story. Congratulations, you can move on to step 2!

2. Gain clarity over your new direction in life and what your first step will be.

Remember it can be a tiptoe, setting time aside to meditate on it, or taking a leap and quitting your job. Not that I necessarily recommend making such an extreme decision right off the bat, but you get the idea. If you can't quite figure out what your first step will be, start with your major concern and address it first. As women, we like to evaluate everything, get educated on it, and take so much time to think about it. We end up jeopardizing ourselves versus simply taking one step forward. So, what is your top concern, and how can we fix it today? If, and I say if, you still can't come up with anything to do, just do something to make yourself happy.

We work with a woman, who was employed by a company that was bought by another company. Shortly after the change in ownership, her position was eliminated, which as you know happens all too often in the corporate world. She is a single woman, no children, and really didn't have to be that accountable with her spending and saving habits. It was just her, after all, so she could spend extravagantly on her cars, vacations, and wardrobe. After she had lost her job, she looked around for a few years trying to find something else to fill the gap before she planned on retiring. She found a few options, but nothing permanent or worth staying around for. And guess what she decided? She decided to change the direction of her life and give up the corporate shuffle and retire. There were a few steps she needed to take for it to happen, though. First, she had to really look at her expenses and start cutting back a bit. She downsized her house and gave up a few other luxuries she knew she didn't need. In the end, what she gained the most was clarity over what she really wanted for the next chapter of her life.

She didn't need the fancy car, big house, or designer wardrobe. What she wanted was to feel confident retiring, secure with her money and money choices, and to know she wouldn't have to go back to work. And she is on her way, all because she made a decision for change, got a plan in place with our help and guidance, and took the necessary steps. And she has us here to help keep her retired and living the life she wants; we are her accountability partners, which leads me to step 3.

3.   Implementing and Being Accountable.

What happens when we say we are going to start going to the gym? But then we say we won't go now; we will go when? LATER. Then your children come home from school, and your husband gets in from a long day of work (why is it always a LONG day for them? We work just as hard!), and you have to cook dinner. Hours later it is eight o'clock at night, and there's still laundry to do and dishes in the sink. Did we ever get to the gym? NOPE!

You need to be accountable, and you need an accountability buddy, someone who will drag your butt to the gym at six in the morning or nine at night. Now, your accountability buddy isn't your husband, or your wife, or best friend. Because the people you are close to (usually) only want to keep you safe and comfortable because we all love being comfortable…even when we know being comfortable isn't helping us. For me, an accountability buddy means someone who will email, call, and text when needed to make sure you get something done. I get it! Life happens, and it tends to get in the way. So, I am there to make sure something important like getting your wills done or upping your liability insurance, isn't overlooked. Or, to keep you on track with your plan, to help get you to your goals.

You can implement your plan by acting today, and you can be accountable by taking repeated action tomorrow and the next day. We focus so much time and energy on all the other aspects of our lives, why can't we set aside a few minutes every week to review our money? What have I been saying all along? *Money affects every aspect of our life.* So, can we all agree to take some time every week and month to focus on one thing that affects EVERYTHING? It is for this exact reason that I set up monthly calls with my clients. It can be so easy to just forget, push it off to the next month, or not feel like doing it. But if you schedule it ahead of time and mark your calendar for it, you will more than likely keep to it.

Here is my Monthly To-Do List I use with my clients:

1. What is your top financial goal for this month?

2. What are you willing to give up for this goal?

3. What big expenses are expected for the month, and how will we address those expenses?

4. How much are you going to save for the month?

5. And lastly, TRACKING! Track your cash flow, your net worth, and your progress toward your goals.

Let's dive into the fifth and probably most important step, tracking. It is so important to know where your money is going, what is affecting it, and if there were any side steps or back steps. What do I mean by this? Take your cash flow, for instance, which is how much money you make, how much you spend, and the net result. Did you spend more than you make? Did you save some money, or were you even for the month? If you are spending more than you make, there is a problem. The next question is: was this a one-time occurrence or does it happen more months than you'd like to admit? If you are saving money, where is that extra money going? To an emergency fund, to retirement savings, or to a specific goal? It is why tracking each month is a necessity for me, because every month is different. You will have unique and different expenses every month, so the only way to find a trend is to track it.

Don't think of tracking like being on a budget. I HATE that word. A budget is like a diet; they are great in the short term but aren't sustainable. This is a lifestyle change, and by tracking your spending, you are really opening your eyes to the choices you do have out there. When you look at your expenses, think about what is important to you. Is it eating out, traveling, or going to concerts? Then maybe you should spend less on an apartment or house, so you have more available funds to do these activities. Or maybe, you'd rather have a nice house or car. If that's the case, then you might have to start doing your own nails or shop less. I read once that you should write down your top ten financial goals in your life, and then pick three. Chances are, you won't have enough money for all of them, so reflect on what really matters to you and start there. Again, it is why knowing what you really want and having clarity over it, can help you prioritize your spending and saving.

Your net worth is just as important. You need to look at your assets, minus your liabilities and see the net result. Are your assets growing because you are adding money or because of investment performance? Are they going down because of investments or because you are depleting them? Are your liabilities decreasing because you are paying them down; are they staying the same, or are they going up as you add more debt to them? And the great part of tracking is that you can see the progress firsthand. It's different than periodically going online and reading a new account value or credit card balance. You see where you began, where you are now, and how much farther you have to go until you hit your goals.

Let me give you an example of the powerful impact tracking can make on your life. One woman I work with was going into debt by about $2,000 a month and was about $30,000 in debt when she DECIDED enough was enough. She was sick of being terrified, overwhelmed, and stressed over her money every day. She felt like a failure to herself, to her children, and to her parents who continued to give her financial support. So, she decided to make a change for her life and for her family's lives.

Through the simple process of implementing monthly tracking, she dramatically adjusted her spending without feeling deprived every month. She is now breaking even every month and is starting to save extra each month as well. She needs to build up her savings, so she won't have to go into debt if a big expense comes up like new tires, a new furnace, or something for her children. We never want to say no to our children, do we? The best part is she feels hope for the first time in over 15 years, and she has a better grasp over her money and happiness. She is happy, less stressed (which is an understatement), more energized, and guess what? Her self-worth is on the rise. She has an all new energy and joy around her. And her net worth is following right in line with her increasing value in herself. Amazing what a little knowledge, hard work, and guidance can do for the soul. I am her accountability buddy, who calls her monthly to make sure she stays on track. Otherwise, she would fall back into her old ways.

Here is your BONUS Monthly To-Do List Worksheet to get you started.

1. Top financial goal:_____

2. Monthly Spending Cleanse*:_____

3. Big expense and estimated cost:_____

4. Savings goal:_____

5. Tracking:_____

    a. Surplus/deficit amount:_____

    b. Total assets:_____ Total debits:_____

        Net worth:_____

    c. Progress toward goals:_____

*Monthly Spending Cleanse is a concept I'm using with my blog, *Not Your Father's Advisor*. Every month I give up one item, which means I will save money anytime I would normally have spent on that item throughout the month. My theory is that anyone can go without one thing for 30 days, especially if it brings you closer to your goals. Here are some examples: no alcohol, no shopping, no eating out, and no manicures/pedicures. My total savings for the first 6 months is about $1,500, which isn't too bad for not altering my life. So, don't say there are no other areas where you can save money; use this as inspiration! One woman saved an extra $10,000 for a bathroom renovation, and the best part is that she doesn't have to use debt now to pay for it. The results from this method are similar to what happens when we eat healthier. We start by giving up one thing like candy. The next month, it is soda, and then no fried food. It's such a small change, but it creates a huge difference in your waistline. What are you willing to give up for just one month to get closer to your goals? And if you want to know what my savings will be going toward, since I am pregnant, the money I save will go toward decorating the nursery. I LOVE decorating, and when I start my project, my husband won't be able to get mad since I will already have saved up the money.

"Dreams and dedication are a powerful combination."
~William Longgood

Everyone dreams of having the life they've always wanted. *Maybe if I win the lottery? Maybe in retirement? Maybe if my children ever leave the nest...* Maybe, but not today, right? The difference between you and all the dreamers, is *you* are acting on your plans. And *you* are dedicated to taking repeated action. What you'll find is a little bit of success. With success, you will start believing in your money mantra, and you will continue to take these small steps, leading you to more success. All along, you will find small victories to celebrate that will keep you going on your way.

You are probably very busy with your life, and might not have the discipline or time to make sure you get it all done. This is where I come in, as your coach, to help get you on track and keep you there. If it isn't me, find someone who wants it as much as you do, and who will do anything they can to make it possible. I call it "learning when to outsource." Outsourcing shouldn't cost you more money, right? It shouldn't if you think about what you could do with your newfound time. Make sure you are more than making up what you are paying for. Or, if you are working with a professional, who earns you more money on your investment, then it should make sense. You could potentially save more money, save money on taxes, earn more money, and get more knowledge overall. And knowledge is power! I encourage every woman I work with to get knowledgeable, and I will educate them along the way. Because even if you are working with a professional, it is critical to know he or she is working in your best interest. Which means…they aren't putting you into products to increase their income. Get what I'm saying? I think so.

To take action, we need to know where we are going. Take some time to think about your life and money goals. Write them down below to keep yourself accountable.

1-Year Life Goals:

_____

_____

_____

1-Year Money Goals:

_____

_____

_____

5-Year Life Goals:

_____

_____

_____

5-Year Money Goals:

_____

_____

_____

10-Year Life Goals:

_____

_____

_____

10-Year Money Goals:

_____

_____

_____

When you use tracking, you will know where you are today, and you will know where you want to be. How do we get there? By having a plan in place with strategies for today, tomorrow, and so on, which brings us to Chapter 5.

Chapter 5: Let's Start Building Your Plan

"Strong women wear their pain like they do stilettos. No matter how much it hurts, all you see is the beauty of it."
~Harriet Morgan

There are times when I will plan for hours on end and other times when I wing my plans only to forget something necessary. Let me give you a few examples. If I have a big event coming up, I will plan my outfit numerous times; I will keep planning it out even if I know what I want to wear, and I will even forget about that outfit and plan another entirely new outfit. I will think about it when I'm driving when I go running, and while I get ready for other events. I get sick of how much time I dedicate to a simple outfit, especially when the outfit turns out to be a terrible combination of pants, top, shoes, and accessories. It's way too embarrassing to admit how long I really thought about it, only to have it turn out to be a disaster, so then I have to haul butt putting together yet another outfit at the last minute. Maybe this isn't the best example of planning. Let me try again.

When I get ready for my morning run, I really put some thought into it. I even map out my whole week of runs, when my easy days will be, moderate days, and hard days, and how far they each will be as well. I know exactly how hard I want it to go (or easy), what my running route is, how long I want it to take me, and so on. If I didn't plan my run, do you think I would really get the most out of it? I'd probably do a mixture of hard and easy, but by the time I would start sprinting, my run would be over. I would be wasting precious running time debating what to do, and it would not be productive at all.

Now, I am a planner by nature. Remember, I grew up with a financial planner as a father and with a mother, who was OCD when it came to organization. (Hopefully, she will never look behind my closet doors or in my home office desk!) But, there are times when I HATE to plan, (hate, despise, avoid, or any other word you can fill in to describe this overwhelming feeling of loathing.) Maybe you are like this with planning out your finances. Don't worry, I've got you covered if that is the case. For me, I HATE planning my trip to the grocery store. It's probably just the fact of hating to go to the grocery store period. Again, you might be just like this when it comes to your money; you avoid it until there is no more food in the fridge or money in your bank account.

Today, for instance, I went to the store, and I clocked how long it took me to get in, pay, and load up my car. It was 26 minutes, whoot whoot! Not too shabby, but I must say, it definitely wasn't one of my better trips. I forgot a handful of items; some I remembered in the store, but I was too far from the aisle, and so they remain in their resting place. I even put somewhat of a list together because we were very low on spices and herbs, which we use a ton of; thank you, Food Network. After all that, I still forgot one of the herbs, a case of water, and a few other items necessary for the meals I'm planning on making. Whether I'm an average or poor cook or not, I still love to cook. And now, because I forgot some items that I needed, I will have to waste extra time during my hectic week to go back to the store and pick them up. I will waste time and probably waste more money because I'm pregnant, and being pregnant at a grocery store means you are guaranteed to buy some sort of snack you never thought was appealing before. Bonus that I probably won't plan out that trip either, so I'll forget one item, and the cycle goes on and on.

You can guess where I'm going with all these planning stories. When we plan and plan right, it can give us incredible results. There will be times, I will warn you when you will plan, and it won't go according to your plan. Why? Because life happens and will throw a curveball at you or a Jimmy Choo shoe at you—to give you a female metaphor. But if we can react to the setback or new lane life presents us with, we can always fall back on our overall plan and get moving again. It always amazes me when people go into a major life transition—say retirement—without putting an ounce of thought into it. It is ONLY the next 20-30 plus years of your life... But hey, why plan it out? Think about your social security strategy. It is a million dollar or more question on when to take it. So, why do what your neighbor, sister, or friend did? No one on this planet has the same exact situation as you, which is why no one should have the same plan in place. You need a custom plan, and we will start building your plan in this chapter.

I will give you a blueprint to follow or your overall GPS. But just like when you are driving to a new destination, you might hit traffic or find a quicker route; you might get a flat tire, or encounter some other interference; don't worry, we *will* get you from point A to point B. But you may find new routes along the way, quicker ones, or maybe there will be times when we need to find longer ones because we need to move a little slower. The point is to keep moving, adjust your plan when necessary, and get to your end goal and destination.

A woman called into our office to ask a "quick question." Her question was when she should take social security. After spending some time with her on the phone, I explained how throughout someone's retirement, questions pop up around every corner. There are so many different ages, penalties, taxes, withdrawals, enrollment periods, income, and expense numbers to think about, answer, and to NOT forget about. I told her that after answering this one quick question, the floodgates would open with more and more questions, and I stressed how important it was to have a plan in place for all of them. It clicked for her all of a sudden, as she said, "That must be why this one question is so daunting to me." It wasn't just the question weighing on her; it was all that went along with it. When to take her pension. When to retire. How much money will she need? How will she pay off her debt? How will she not get back into debt? How much will health insurance cost? If she would need to sell her house and so on. I could tell it was all a burden on her since she called our office three other times with the same question. Eventually, she came in for a strategy session and became one of my CFOs in my mentorship program.

We have these questions and don't even realize when there is something deeper troubling us. I see it all the time; it might just be how much to put away for retirement. Women ask me this constantly, and keep asking me every time we meet: *are you sure I'm putting away enough*? It usually is an amount more than just what an extra $100 of savings will do for them. They're terrified to lose their job; they're scared their health may make them retire early, or they might need time off to take care of a loved one. Our first questions and concerns come from the surface, and what we really are terrified of when it relates to our money is beneath all these questions. *Will I get through this? Will I be okay? Will I ever be happy again? Will I ever find peace?*

During a strategy session with a single mother, we discovered some of these hidden concerns and fears. We had met to go through her strategy for the next 10 years as her children started going off to college, and she was able to put some much-needed focus back on herself and her finances. Turned out, she was terrified she was making one bad financial decision after another, and the impacts of her decisions were so unnerving to her. Because they wouldn't just affect her life, but her daughters' lives as well. What if she made a bad decision and had no idea of the consequences of that decision 5 years or 10 years down the road?

What if she stayed in her big house and had to go into debt to keep up their lifestyle? There were too many what-ifs swirling around in her brain, keeping her up at night. We started talking about what she wants to discard from her life and got to the root of what she desired for this next chapter. What is it that she really wants now that she is divorced and her children are away at college? She didn't want her huge house anymore, instead, what she really wanted was to feel more secure and confident with her choices. She hoped for more time to travel with her family, and more income to save for her retirement, so she wouldn't be dependent on her ex's alimony. We went through the strategies to get her there and identified what behaviors to change and modify to get her on the path to happiness. Her confidence to take action grew as we put her plan into place. She was able to visualize all her choices to learn what really made sense for her and what she ended up wanting for her life down the road. As she started to change her beliefs to believe she could accomplish what she had outlined and discovered the will do, she started changing her behaviors, too, which has led to some success. Your plan is vital to your success, to taking action, to following through, and to continuing on **your** path. I'm **only** here to help you create your plan and your path.

We built her plan by implementing what we've already talked about in the beginning chapters. To make sure you're on your own path, here are the steps I recommend using that comprise a surefire way women I work with every day are implementing to get over their money fears:

Step 1: Decide what it is you want. Let's take a moment to envision what you want for your life. I recommend booking a **Discovery Call** with me to do this very thing, to help you discover what you want for your life and what is stopping you from getting it. What can we do to get you financially secure and give you the freedom of choices with your money? Doesn't that sound nice? You will have to start realigning your beliefs to match what you want. If you believe you will never get out of debt, well, guess what? You never will. You can start a new mantra by saying, "I will live debt free." Or, if you're worried about funding your retirement, start believing *I will have a bountiful retirement*. Again, **Step 1** is to book a call with me. It can't get much easier than that!

Step 2: Discover what your current money behaviors are doing for you and your goals. If you believe you will never get out of debt, then you are probably engaging in behaviors to make sure you stay in debt. If you are nervous about having enough money for retirement, then you are probably not saving enough. Our behaviors mirror our beliefs so that our beliefs come to fruition. Knowing this, why don't we change our beliefs and behaviors, so we actually get what we want? **Step 2** is to create a plan or a strategy to get your behaviors in line with your new beliefs. Simple, huh? **Step 2**, in my world, is a **Strategy Session** to establish where you are today, where you want to go, and to figure out how we will get you there. Great, you've had your **Discovery Call** and gone through your **Strategy Session**, so now, it's on to **Step 3**.

Step 3: Wow, you are already on **Step 3,** awesome! Congratulations for getting here!! Do a little dance, pop open a bottle of champagne, and celebrate your victory. Now that we have a plan, what must we do? IMPLEMENT and TRACK it. We celebrated a little, but now it is time to get down to business. I will be honest; this is where most people fall short. They have every intention of putting their plan to work, but they get busy with life, or they procrastinate. To help you get on track and stay there, it is a huge benefit to have an accountability buddy. Someone to push you along the way, to go to for advice or maybe just to vent to, and more importantly, to guide you through the hiccups and roadblocks.

For you or anyone going through a transition, you will need two plans: 1) your short term, "HELP get me through this" plan, and 2) your new chapter plan. Sound about right? Someone going through a divorce might not be able to set up their retirement accounts, start saving, and begin to pay down debt, etc. If this is you, you will just need a way to get yourself through the divorce with as few scars as possible. OR maybe you are changing careers. There are things you can start doing while still at your old job, but nothing life-altering yet. For instance, you can do research on your new industry and find the field in that industry that will make you happy and give you satisfaction.

If you are suddenly single from losing a spouse or from divorce, you will need to address the immediate things necessary to continue moving forward each day. It might be to just climb out of bed every morning to get your children to school. Your everyday tasks will seem insurmountable, and you will have added the increased responsibilities of being both mom and dad. What will help is getting your support system in place: the people who can help and learning when they can help. Don't be too modest to ask for help; now is the time to cash in on those offers. Support can be in the form of friends, therapists, family members, and professionals. I remember my good friend describing her support system during her divorce as an analogy with each friend playing a role. She knew who to go to when she needed to blow off steam, who to go to for advice, and my favorite, who to go to when her temper flared—the enraged comrade—who is just as pissed off as you are.

You can rely on a group of professionals in the same fashion, a therapist to vent to, an advisor to get advice from and put a plan in place, and an attorney for all the legal matters. It's a similar situation if you lose your husband; the same support group of friends and family and the same group of professionals can all help you get through it. One client, whose husband and mother were both terminally ill at the same time, had one child in college and another who was a senior in high school. Her son needed to start looking at colleges, and her brother-in-law and sister-in-law took him on trips to different schools. Our lives and our family's lives don't get put on hold until we emerge out of a tough time, and having support can get you and your family through it in the best way possible. Your support is there to pick up the pieces, make sure nothing major is forgotten, and to get you managing again, maybe even with a laugh or two down the road.

During these transitions, a checklist can be one of the best ways to make sure you tackle one thing every day or week. Write down what needs to be addressed immediately, and what can wait until a little later. Bills will still need to get paid; taxes will be owed, documents will need updating, and health insurance changed. Find out how long you have to change your coverage and go from there. If you need to continue your health insurance coverage, you might be covered through COBRA for 18, 29, or 36 months. While it does cost a pretty penny for the insurance coverage, it might be worth it in your case. If you need some time off during your transition, you might qualify for the federal Family and Medical Leave Act (FMLA.) Here is some more information on it since most people I've spoken with don't know about it or the workings of it.

Because of a recent interview with a client, I found out about the federal Family and Medical Leave Act. Her husband had lung cancer, and at the same time, her mother needed round-the-clock care. Her family was in New Jersey, but her mother and father were in Mississippi, so she was pulled in a lot of different directions. Luckily, she had an understanding and flexible employer, who let her work remotely a good amount of the time. However, there were still other times when she needed more time off from work. This is when she found out about the Family and Medical Leave Act.

Here is a summary of the act from the website: https://www.dol.gov/whd/fmla/

"The FMLA entitles eligible employees of covered employers to take unpaid, job-protected leave for specified family and medical reasons with continuation of group health insurance coverage under the same terms and conditions that would apply if the employee had not taken leave. Eligible employees are entitled to:

12 workweeks of leave in a 12-month period for:

o   the birth of a child and to care for the newborn child within one year of birth;

o   the placement with the employee of a child for adoption or foster care and to care for the newly-placed child within one year of placement;

- o to care for the employee's spouse, child, or parent who has a serious health condition;

- o a serious health condition that makes the employee unable to perform the essential functions of his or her job;

- o any qualifying exigency arising out of the fact that the employee's spouse, son, daughter, or parent is a covered military member on "covered active duty;" **or**

- 26 workweeks of leave during a single 12-month period to care for a covered service member with a serious injury or illness if the eligible employee is the service member's spouse, son, daughter, parent, or next of kin (military caregiver leave.)"

And please make sure your money and finances are taken care of while you take some time off work, too. Just because you take a leave from work, doesn't mean you take a leave from your finances. Having a plan in place can give you more comfort than you would have had otherwise before you had no choice but to take time off work. You can then put all your focus into helping your loved ones and not worrying. Wouldn't that be nice? I can't stress it enough; *your work may be placed on hold, but your goals don't have to be.* There will be many elements to your plan, and I've found the best way to start putting them all together is to go through a checklist of all the fun financial factors!

So, let's look at the other areas of finances to start building your short-term and long-term plans. You can mark each component you need to address and use it as a blueprint to your plan.

1. Debt: How does debt factor into your goal?

a. Use it to purchase a house, car, etc.?

    i. What type of loan to get? Will there be tax benefits with certain types of loans such as a home equity loan?

b. Pay it down?

    i. If so, how much debt do you have? What are the interest rates you are paying? Find the highest interest rate and start there. How will you pay it down more quickly or how much extra can you pay each month to lower it?

c. How to prevent debt?

    i. Building up an emergency fund or having a plan in place when large, unexpected expenses come up can really help. Grow your savings to prevent having to use your credit card if your refrigerator breaks or you need a new roof, for example.

d. Good debt versus bad debt. In our society, we seem to always go to our credit cards first; it's just so easy. I think savings is a lost art; when we want something, we want it NOW! So, we take out our credit card, and it's fine until you start quickly spending more than you make. If you are constantly carrying a balance on your credit cards each month, there might be a problem, and then you should go back to bullet b. We need debt to buy a house, build a startup company, and to buy a car sometimes. These are all forms of good debt because they are building us wealth (hopefully) and are viewed as investments. Bad debt stems from living a lifestyle above our pay grade. It's due to spending recklessly on clothing, vacations, really good wines, and things we don't need. Does your plan involve using good debt to build your wealth or getting rid of bad debt, which prevents you from growing your wealth?

2. Savings: I'm sure we could all use a little more savings.

   a. Growing your savings: do you need to grow your savings to get to your goals?

      i. If so, by how much each year? Then you can break it down to each month and each week. How will you increase your savings? Will you make more money or spend less or a combination of both? Look through your expenses to see what you can easily cut out, what you are willing to cut out, and determine if there is still a shortfall. Can you ask for a raise, go for a new job or promotion, work longer hours, or earn some money on the side? Women tend to be reluctant to ask for a raise or go for a promotion. My friend, who worked in human resources for years at a large corporation, said exactly this. She would see guy after guy asking for a large raise while the women (herself included) were too scared to go for it. Remember what your self-worth is, and what your value is to the company, then ASK! If they say no, you are in the same spot you were before. Try asking what the company's top concern or challenge is, and see if you can address it. That will be more valuable to them than you can ever imagine.

b. Maybe you are on the flip side and need to start withdrawing from your savings. If you are about to purchase something or are in retirement, you will be reducing your savings. What is the best way to do this? How much should you withdraw so you won't run out of money?

    i. Think of your savings in three buckets of money: your short-term bucket, medium-term bucket, and long-term bucket. Your short-term bucket is for your immediate needs that will arise within the next 1 to 3 years and should be managed conservatively. Whereas, you can handle your long-term bucket more aggressively because you won't need the money for 20 plus years.

3. Investments, my favorite! How can your money work just as hard as you do?

a. Please do not hoard all your money in the bank! Of course, keep some money in a bank account as your emergency fund, (about 3 months of expenses.) Some say 6 months of expenses, but if you remember, we have 3 buckets of money for your investments. Therefore, if bucket number 1 is invested very conservatively, you will be fine with only 3 months, and you will have the potential to earn more than what the measly bank accounts are now paying. Yes, I said it! It is horrible how much people are losing due to inflation just by keeping the bulk of their money in a bank account. If inflation is 3 percent, and your money is earning 1 percent, what is your actual return? A negative 2 percent; that means you are **losing** the purchasing power or value of your money by 2 percent each year.

b. When you put together an investment strategy, make sure it is aligned with your risk tolerance, account objective, and time horizon for your goals. Here is a breakdown of how they all work together:

Everyone is different, and it keeps the world interesting, and it keeps me on my toes with my clients. One of the most crucial exercises we do with everyone we work with is to go through their risk tolerance assessment and then review it every year. Anything can happen in a year, and people's circumstances change. As we know, the only constant in this world is change. Well whenever someone's situation gets adjusted, or they get closer to their financial goals, they tend to switch their objectives for their investments as well as their risk tolerances.

An account objective can be growth-oriented, income-driven, concern capital preservation, or anything in between. Think of the growth objective on the more aggressive side of the spectrum and capital preservation on the conservative side. So, where do you match up? Ha! That is a loaded question, and most people don't even know what their true objective is or if their accounts have even been invested according to their objectives. Now, before we dive into how to accomplish this proper alignment, let's go through your risk tolerance because they go hand in hand.

Your risk tolerance, or pain threshold as I like to call it, shows how much risk you are willing to take for more of a **POTENTIAL** return. No returns are guaranteed, so potential is as bold as I can make it. Most people initially say, "Sure, let's take on a lot of risk because I want my money to grow and grow fast." But can you guess what happens? Well, the stock market has one of their 10-percent pullbacks, and suddenly, that growth-minded risk-taker stops dead in their tracks. *Wait a second; I wanted growth, not for my account to go down by 10 percent.* Well, I would like to know where you can get 20 percent gains without it ever going down, and please let me know if you possess this secret. So, this is where the account objective and risk tolerance cross paths.

You see when you want growth, you have growth-oriented investments, but then when the market goes down, sometimes, you freak out and want to change gears. When I say, "change gears," I mean you go from an aggressive allocation to a very conservative one. So, now your account's investments don't match up with your actual long-term objective because your silly old risk tolerance got in the way. You thought you were a high-risk, high-reward type of person, but now it seems you are a low-risk; give-me-whatever returns-I-can-get type of person. And this is exactly why we need to re-evaluate your investment objective and risk tolerance every year. It works the same when you have a low-risk tolerance, conservative account objective, and the market goes sky high. And then you will ask the question, "Why isn't my account up as much as the stock market?" Since we don't live in a perfect world, and we are always changing and adjusting our lives, it is critical to do 2 things with your investments.

1. Make sure your investments match your objectives, risk tolerance, and time horizon, right off the bat.

2. Make sure to review the above every year, and periodically, as your world changes.

> Think of it this way; you really want a house on the beach. A house right on the beach with gorgeous ocean views from every room. You know there have been storms before that have brought water into the house, damaged parts of the house, yet it is still your dream. So, you start looking at real estate and find the perfect one. It happens to be in your budget, YAY!!

Knowing the risks associated with owning a house on the beach (Super Storm Sandy), you put in an offer, and it gets accepted. Your first summer is amazing; you have all your family and friends down and create loads of memories. There are a few setbacks along the way, such as buying all new furniture and all the entertaining means more money, so it is an expensive first summer. To you, it is still worth the extra money, time, and energy keeping up a beach house. Then in the winter, a huge storm hits. Your full-time home is about two hours away from the beach house, so you don't make it there immediately to see the damage. By the time you get to your dream house, there is water throughout the downstairs. *Uh-oh, this can't be happening*! Well, it has, and you knew the risk when you bought it. So, do you start repairing what needs to be done, with the aim that it will be ready by the summer or do you sell it at a loss? Do you remember why you bought it in the first place and what your long-term goals are? Now you might say, "That is what insurance is for," and to that, I will reply, "There are insurance-type products for your investments, too."

Think of the stock market in the same way. You become invested and it just so happens to go up a few weeks in a row, then a few months, and you are living the life. Your goals are that much closer! But soon, the setbacks hit, such as Britain leaving the EU, the FED raising interest rates, and another one of President Trump's tweets that send the markets downward. Nothing major, you are in it for the long haul, right? Until finally, there is a bigger pullback that leaves you scratching your head. You know the market goes down from time to time, and actually, it averages a 5-10 percent pullback each year, yet it still hurts when it's your money. Back to the dilemmas. Do you sell the beach house or your stocks? Or do you remember your long-term goals and stay put?

I can't answer this for you, but hopefully, it puts the next stock market pullback into perspective a little bit. It is my job to guide you along the way, and try to help you (I said try) put your emotions on the sidelines during your decision-making process. I know it can be very hard, but making a choice while emotional tends to lead to rash decisions. I will leave you with a tip to review your objectives, risk tolerance, and time horizon before you invest and throughout your investing future.

c. Now women have gotten a bad rap on investing, and I would like to debunk the myth right now. Men undertake their investments with complete faith in what they know and what they want to accomplish. They attack their finances the same way women tackle stilettos. Women will coddle their investment portfolio and tend to be timid when making changes. In the financial world, men show overconfidence, and women are inclined to be self-doubting with their decisions. First, let's see whether this is something only I've noticed if it's a notable development or a complete myth.

In BlackRock's latest 2014 Investor Pulse survey, 54 percent of men are confident in their investment decisions versus only 34 percent of women[3]. Many studies have been performed to find out the reason for the difference between our conviction levels. But why does this pattern exist? What in our genetic makeup creates this difference in how women and men think?

A study by John Coates, who is a former Wall Street Trader, shows that "...a connection between testosterone and risk-taking leads to irrational exuberance." This link influences men into trading 45 percent more in their portfolios than women do.

The "irrational exuberance" intensifies when markets are going down[4]. I must say this makes a lot of sense, and can probably be applied to other areas of life. Women, on the other hand, favor investments with guarantees; remember we like to coddle our portfolios just like our children. They prefer to stay away from stock market volatility and invest in CDs and short-term bonds.

—

[3]Aleks Todovora, "What Men Can Learn From Female Investors," http://money. usnews. com/money/blogs/the-smarter-mutual-fund-investor/2015/02/24/what-men-can-learn-from-female-investors, (February 24, 2015)

[4]Lisa Smith, "Women and Investing: It's A Style Thing," http://www. investopedia. com/articles/investing/031313/women-and-investing-its-style-thing. asp

However, there isn't much growth with these "safe" investments. Between taxes and inflation, you are left with a small rate of return, if any.

Even women who have taken the more conservative route with "safe" investments have done better than men. It is during the periods of large market fluctuations when women have outperformed.

Studies executed on gender differences and behavioral investing show that women have consistently achieved better results[5]. Women like to invest in conservative investments; therefore, they do well in periods of market instability. We take more time with our investment and financial decisions because we like to fully understand all our options. This is not necessarily a bad way to behave, and more likely, it's a better way to analyze new ideas. Maybe it is a sign of confidence to say we don't know enough about this investment to make a quick decision.

As investors, we should embrace our feminine strengths while overcoming insecurities in our financial confidence.

———

[5]Lisa Smith, "Women and Investing: It's A Style Thing," http://www. investopedia. com/articles/investing/031313/women-and-investing-its-style-thing. asp

    d. Go ahead and find out all your options and how they can work for you and their impacts.

      Get educated even if you are already working with a professional because you want to make sure what they are doing really is in your best interests.

4. Documents: it is time to get some updating done! Just like we need to update our wardrobe from time to time, we need to update our wills, power of attorneys, living wills, and beneficiaries. If you are newly divorced, I do not think you want your ex-spouse to receive your estate or make a life-altering decision for you if you are in a coma.

    a. Let's dive into beneficiary reviews a little more:

        i. What does beneficiary review entail? To start with, you should track down your 401(k) statements, your IRA statements, your life insurance policies, any annuity statements, and any other account that has a beneficiary designation. Next, simply check the primary and contingent beneficiary designations for all accounts. You may have to go online to view who the beneficiary is, but you probably will have to go online anyway to update it. While some sites may offer a simple option to log into your account, most of them will need a form, so YAY more paperwork! I'll go through a few life or work changes that may prompt you to revisit both your beneficiary designations and your estate planning documents.

If any of your 401(k)s have changed to a different custodian, such as from Vanguard to Fidelity, you should double check your beneficiary designation. We've seen multiple instances where a designation hasn't transferred over. You may have even added the beneficiaries several times, but they never seem to show up on your account or statements. If this is the case, contact your HR department or the custodian to get something in writing listing the name of your beneficiary. It took one widow 16 months to get her husband's 401(k) check because her name wasn't listed. She finally got the 401(k) check since the company had the proper information on a form, but it was with the old custodian. Unfortunately, she still had bills to pay along with her mortgage, so 16 months was a long time to go without that money. Apparently, the cable company won't care if you're waiting on a 401(k) check.

When you start having children, make sure you update all your documents. Many couples will update the beneficiary on their accounts when they have their first child, but then they forget to add their second or third child. What happens in this case? Do your directives go according to your will? Nope, only the child listed will inherit the 401(k), and trust me; you don't want to assume they will split it with their siblings. Nor do you want to put them in such a situation. Too many families have been broken up over money and estate issues.

What if you are recently divorced? Yes, you better revisit your beneficiary designations. Now if you have updated your will post-divorce, do your 401(k)s, life insurance, and IRAs go according to your will? Your IRAs and life insurance will if you live in New Jersey, so please check what your state law says. Any ERISA retirement plans, such as your 401(k), will go according to your beneficiary designation. And you'd probably rather the money go to a stranger before it goes to your ex-spouse, just guessing.

You can have a bank account or a non-retirement investment account with a beneficiary designation, also known as a Transfer On Death account (TOD account) or Payable On Death account (POD account.) If you would like to add this to any account, ask your bank or financial advisor. They should all be able to do this for your accounts. These can come in handy if you are taking care of an elderly parent. If they pass away, the money will go directly to you to help pay any hospital or medical bills.

When you have your beneficiary designations updated and filled in, your estate will most likely save time and money. Any asset or account that has a beneficiary designation bypasses probate since the rule is according to the designation and not your will. Any money that transfers outside of probate is kept private and away from creditors. Leaving certain assets to your loved ones and not to your estate will probably save on income taxes as well. Assets, such as a retirement plan, can be passed onto your family and kept in an Inherited IRA or a Spousal IRA. Doing so allows them to keep the money in a tax-deferred vehicle versus taking all the money out and paying income taxes on all or most of it. But first, you should know you must take Required Minimum Distributions each year if you roll money into an Inherited or Beneficiary IRA. As always, speak with an estate attorney and accountant to find the best way to pass on your money to your family, friends, or charities.

b. To recap, make sure you review your will, power of attorney, and living will along with ALL your beneficiary designations. It isn't morbid to think about your estate; it is critical you do it. And I like to encourage you to reward yourself with a martini or piece of decadent chocolate cake after you have; just make sure it's something strong. It isn't a fun topic to think about, and most people avoid it. Don't be one of those people. You are stronger than that, remember?

5. Family Protection: We call insurance *family protection* because who do we want to protect more than anything? Our family. Insurance will help you do it.

Here is a checklist with some questions to think about as you go through your various insurance policies.

a. **Health Insurance:**

i. Is COBRA available? If so, for how long?

ii. What are the costs for your plan versus a spouse's plan?

iii. Is it worth it to spend less each month for a watered-down policy?

iv. Any big health-related expenses coming up or surgeries?

b. **Disability Insurance:**

    i. Do you pay out-of-pocket or does your employer? There are tax benefits if you pay.

    ii. What does it cover? Are overtime or commissions included?

    iii. How much will it pay out? It might be a good idea to see if you can apply for more coverage with a private plan.

c. **Home and Auto:**

    i. What is your liability amount? Think about upping the amount.

    ii. Do you have an umbrella policy? If not, you can add $1 million, $2 million, or more of extra coverage to your home and auto plans. We do live in the land of lawsuits remember! I highly recommend an umbrella policy if you have significant assets or children driving.

d. **Long-Term Care:**

    i. Are you over the age of 60 and still healthy? Maybe it is time to start planning for long-term care costs.

    ii. There are new and inventive ways to get long-term care coverage without a traditional plan.

e. **Life Insurance:**

    i. Are your policies all still in-force?

    ii. What type of policies do you have? Term or permanent such as whole life, variable life, universal life, or variable universal life? If you have term, how much longer will your policy be in place? If you have a permanent policy, is it adequately funded? Being adequately funded means your policy will still be in place for your loved ones in the future.

    iii. Has your health improved? You might reduce your premium if it has.

    iv. Is your coverage adequate? No one has ever complained about having too much death benefit; it is always the opposite. What do you want your legacy to be?

As I've always said, "No one ever complained of having too much death benefit on their loved ones. It's been when there has been very little or none that the family became resentful." Please don't leave your family in a bad financial situation. Put some time and money into planning, so you will always be remembered the proper way. It was a very sad story when I sat next to a woman on a plane, whose son had passed away. He left a family of four behind, and he didn't do any estate planning before it happened. Why?

Because we never think it will happen to us, or we just don't want to think about it. But we have to when we have a family to care for, don't we? There wasn't any life insurance on him, and his family was left with a large mortgage, other debt, and three children in college with no way of paying the high tuitions. As a result, the children left school owing a ton in student loans, and they are now bitter that their father didn't do any planning. They asked their grandmother, "If dad cared about us so much, why didn't he plan for his death?" Be the hero your family thinks you are even when you are no longer here. Set them up properly so they can continue with their lives and remember you each step of the way.

Go back through your plan and write down the items you marked. This is your plan blueprint, which will guide you through your transition and propel you into your new life. It is always worth it to do some planning, find your path and put it into action no matter what hurdle you have in front of you. There will be times in your life when a new roadblock or curveball is thrown your way. How you react in those moments will determine if you continue on your path or get sidetracked. OR worse, get stuck. In the next chapter, we will go through how our reactions are even more important than all the planning we can do. Reactions start with attitude. If we are constantly looking for some reason to stop us from following our path, then guess what will happen? Any little raindrop will keep you from your dreams. BUT if we look for the silver lining in what the world throws at us, we will **thrive**. You are too strong not to thrive, and I will show you how to find the positive when you just want to crawl into a dark closet. You will thrive because you are worth it!

Chapter 6: Transitioning from One Version of Yourself to Another

"The strongest actions for a woman are to love herself, be herself, and shine amongst those who never believed she could." ~Unknown

My friend and I were talking about life's many changes and surprises the other day. The women I primarily work with are going through major life changes, but it does seem around every corner, that we encounter a new change. Whether it is a change we were after or not. I went from being a married woman working in the family business to being pregnant and going after my own business. And before long, I will be a mother. These are all examples of changes I pursued. On the other hand, my friend didn't choose her changes. She went from being an employed, married woman to an employed widow to an unemployed widow. Talk about some major changes in her life, all within a year. She was going down one path when suddenly, she had to figure out a whole new way to live for herself and her daughters. Some people, choose to let the past dictate the rest of their lives and don't allow themselves to move on. My friend was not one of them, and you are not either, or you wouldn't be reading my book right now.

If we let these roadblocks and forks in the road keep us stuck and unable to grow from them, then who wins? You always have a choice; you might not be able to choose to bring your husband back or your job back, but you have a choice concerning how you react to it. My friend stood strong, took control over the money and the house, and though she might not have believed she could do it at the time, she still did it. She took action. She now has two amazing daughters, with some grandchildren on the way soon, and an awesome marketing business she started all on her own. She chose not to live in the tough times of her life forever. Instead, she decided her life is worth living, and not just for herself but for her daughters. They now have a role model to look up to, and their children will as well.

It wasn't always easy for her; some family and friends kept saying, "Oh, you'll find another husband to take care of you." Well, she didn't want another husband, nor did she need one to take care of her. At first, she was scared, but then she found she could do everything her husband had done around the house and more.

When we are put in a situation, we can either give up or thrive. Thrive is what she did. We both concluded at the end of our conversation that if you decide your life is worth living and react encouragingly, then you can come out an even better version of yourself. Give yourself some credit; you CAN do it!

The best way to put it:

"She understood that the hardest times in life to go through were when you were transitioning from one version of yourself to another." ~Sarah Addison Allen

My friend and her husband had a plan; they had life goals, but they didn't come to fruition. A new scenario came into her life, and she had to create a fresh plan and goals. It is all about your reactions when life doesn't go as originally planned. You can be upset and never able to move on with your life, or you can use it to find a new version of yourself, one you didn't even know you had in you. You can become a newer and better version of your old self. My friend explained that her husband wouldn't even recognize the woman she is today. I've seen the same thing occur in other women who have reacted as she did. They become the old version of themselves, but not quite, because they've grown, become more confident and independent, as well as more secure with who they are. They value their lives. They value their relationships, and they embrace life's many changes more than they ever have.

Let me put it another way. Your investment account didn't grow like you had planned. What do you do? Throw your plan away, take all your money out, and put it under your mattress? I've seen that happen hundreds of times, too, and the most common emotion afterward is regret. There will always be time to re-evaluate your plan, adjust it, and get on your way again. But to regularly throw out a plan because it didn't go the way you wanted isn't a good idea. You will constantly start from scratch, and you'll probably drag your feet from all the extra work you've just added.

Some people come in to see us, and they are 5 years away from when they **want** to retire. They just can't keep working where they are employed and are trying to figure out how to get out in one piece. They might not have saved enough money to retire in 5 years; maybe 10 years is a feasibility, but not 5 years. Half of my clients get stuck in the past and can't stop talking about their what-ifs. What if they had known more back then? What if they had saved more? What if they hadn't spent so much along the way, and what if they had made better investments? In the end, it is all hindsight bias, and you can either get stuck in the past like they have or be like the other half, who acknowledge they don't have enough money but who still decide to do **something** about it.

Our lives are the result of the choices we've made in the past, and we can either let those choices control us or break free of them. We can decide to live more constructively going forward and react more positively. My mother is a great example of making a conscious decision to not let her childhood affect her future family life. She worked so hard to create an amazing childhood for me and my brother and was able to relive her childhood through us. We went to museums, zoos, amusement parks, and picnics. I honestly don't remember a day where we didn't have some sort of excursion or activity planned.

So many people can get stuck in their negative past. And just because you decide to move forward doesn't mean you miss your husband any less or you weren't affected by the tough moment in your life. It simply means you are using it as a building block in your life to propel yourself to a stronger and better version of yourself. These tough times are what make us who we are. Now, there will be periods in your life where you will feel stuck, lost, or confused. During those moments, it can be beneficial to reflect on your life and your values, and it can help to remember your plan to get to your goals.

If there are times when I feel stuck or confused, I take some time to reflect. *Do I really want whatever it is I am working for?* Will it help me on my way to transform more women's lives? Sometimes the answer is no, and I have to re-evaluate what will get me to the next step. And there are other times when the answer is yes, but I might get a little sidetracked or too complacent. We do get complacent at times, even the overly-ambitious me does. But I know if I stay complacent for too long, I will start to get bored and unhappy at work again. Therefore, it is critical to take the time to really contemplate what I am doing and what I need to do to keep impacting more women. As my father pointed out, I can't work with everyone on a one-on-one basis, BUT with my blog and book, I can reach more women. I can help more women than I've ever thought possible. And that is what keeps me going when I get stuck, complacent, or a little lost.

When you get fixated on a certain step, take some time to reflect like I do. When you are hit with a roadblock, step aside and think about it. Don't rush into it. Remember when we rush into a decision we tend to make a rash or bad choice. And the choice we made in a hurry will only give a brief satisfaction. Give yourself some breathing room to really identify the options that will give you the results you want, and then consider the impacts of those options. Maybe the roadblock is trying to tell you something; you could be rushing your plan or moving in a direction you don't really want to go. If you are dragging your feet, chances are you don't really want to go in the direction you are facing. If that is the case, then you won't ever really commit to your choice or get the results you want.

If you find yourself in the past and examining your what-ifs, use my checklist to help move through the past and into the present:

- Surround yourself with positive and optimistic people. Negative people will only drag you down and keep you there, so you will have to break free of them. Negative people bring out the negative in us whereas, positive people bring out the positive. Plus, you don't want any more drama in your life, so get rid of them. Sorry to be a little harsh, but it is imperative that you have a good support system in place with positive people who can help you to move forward to all the amazing moments to come in your life.

- Give yourself 10 minutes a day to grieve or feel sad, but then move on with your day. Each week, lower the amount of time by a minute until you no longer have any time designated to living in the past. If, throughout the day, your mindset drifts back to the what-ifs, put your thought into a "negativity bubble" again and visualize it sailing away from you. Say to yourself; *I don't need this negativity in my life*!

- Remember, you can stay bitter, resentful, sad, and mad but it will only prevent you from moving forward. Every day you have a choice to live in the past or live in the present. When you wake up, decide how you are going to live your day. If you have a family to support, think of them when you make your decision. You have to be able to live with yourself and your decisions, so the best way to prevent regretting your current choices is to STOP living in the past.

One woman, I interviewed during the process of writing this book, had one of the best attitudes I've ever encountered. She has been through two divorces; both brought her difficult times including no child support, verbal abuse, and so much more. She actually still lives with her second ex-husband as she gets her career going and to help support her children since she travels so much for work. It obviously isn't what she wants for her life now, but she is working so hard to keep moving forward, earn more money, and to give her children a better life. If she let herself get bitter and resentful during her two divorces and afterward as well, she would not be able to move out of any of it. It would keep her in the past and prevent her from moving on, which she knows isn't healthy for her or her children.

She constantly put her children and their needs first during her divorces, and she put her health and mindset second to them. She didn't want to fight for the children's sake, but also for her own sanity. She knows there are more important aspects of her life where she can dedicate her energy. She didn't fight for alimony, not that I recommend this or don't recommend it, but she knew she could channel more money into her life through her hard work. Again, it wasn't worth it to fight; she just preferred moving past the divorce so she wouldn't be stuck in her life. She valued her life and her children's lives way too much to remain in the past. Doing so, allowed her to live for the present and to prepare for her future. When we live in the past, we jeopardize our present and future.

Throughout our interview, she kept reiterating that the importance of one's mindset is all about how we react to things. How much do you love yourself and value your life? Your answer will help dictate which direction you choose to live when you wake up. This woman valued her life too much to let any setback affect her, and I'm sure you do, too!

So, how does it all apply to our money and finances? Unfortunately, I think we value our money even more than we value our health. Because we value our money so highly, we tend to be very emotional about it and probably react too much to it. Don't shake your head as if this isn't true; I do it, too. WE all do it. And our reactions tend to be quick and a bit on the rash side. When we are overly emotional and make a rash decision, what does it leave you with? A bad decision, as I've said, and it doesn't just apply to money, it applies to all areas of your life. But let's look deeper at what can happen when we make a rash decision based on our emotions with money.

After the 2008 financial crisis, most of America woke up with huge declines in their investment accounts, and by huge, I mean 30-45 percent declines[6].

Some left their investments where they were; some took out their money at the bottom of the stock market's decline, and some took their money but never invested it back. They've missed years of potential gains back on their money and have lost money due to inflation. When you put your money in the bank, remember you are losing the purchasing power or the value of your money as inflation goes up.

I remember one woman in particular who withdrew all her family's money after they lost hundreds of thousands of dollars during the crash. Six years later, she finally decided to invest a small portion of their money into the stock market. Although she knew her investments were positioned for the long haul—10 plus years—she reacted the same way she had before when she'd experienced her first stock market correction or pullback.

Once again, she responded very quickly and emotionally to what was happening with her money. Guess she didn't learn her lesson. I remember her explaining how it seemed the entire stock market knew she was investing again, and they'd all decided to screw her over once more. You can see how we let our emotions get the best of us and make us think negatively on aspects we can't even control. You and I can't control what the stock market does, but we can control how we react to it.

—

[6]Nick Gogery, "A Look at Hedge Fund Performance in 2008, 2009," https://seekingalpha. com/article/181786-a-look-at-hedge-fund-performance-in-2008-2009, (January 10, 2010).

How about thinking *the market is down, maybe I should invest more money since it is cheaper to buy stocks now?*

She didn't think this way since she was so paralyzed in the past and it was because of the past that she reacted in the same way. Investing is one area of life where we don't want a discount. I ask, "Why not?" "Why not buy a stock because it went down?" I'm not saying to buy every stock that goes down, but they don't all go down because the company is failing.

Do you see how when we remain in our past mistakes that we threaten our future decisions? It can be a dangerous cycle since we are talking about your life and your money. We are in the positions in our lives now because of the choices we've made in the past. But everything in our lives is a choice, so we can decide how to react differently than we've done in the past to get to a better place for us and for our families.

Life is 10 percent what happens to us and 90 percent how we react to it.

How will you react when the storm clouds of life come up? One woman, we'd just started working with had recently lost her husband. She has three teenage children to take care of on top of the financial mess her husband left her. She never took care of the money when he was alive, so she's been avoiding her finances ever since he passed away. Fortunately, she has a great brother, who brought her to her first appointment with us. She was very quiet during our meeting, didn't ask one question, but later, her brother called us with dozens of concerns his sister had expressed to him. If she'd only spoken up during our meeting, we could have addressed all of them, which would have helped her and we would have given her more value. It has now been two months since our meeting, and we are finally getting closer to creating her plan.

After countless emails and phone calls to her, we realized the only way to get through to her is by talking with her brother. She has simply passed the finance torch from her husband to her brother. She doesn't want to be on any of the phone calls or meetings; she only wants her brother to relay messages to her. As you have come to know me by now; I'm sure you realize I was not happy with this plan. If we are dealing with your money, we need to talk with you. It is the only way we can have a trusting and long-lasting relationship together. Instead of reacting to her situation, she is avoiding it and diverting it to her brother, which is only adding to his workload.

There are a good number of women who like to let their husbands manage all the money. If we can even get them to come into the office for a meeting or talk to them on the phone, they sit there quietly. I am not judging you if you like to do this exact thing; there are things my husband does that are important but I don't get involved with, like maintaining our house. Something I, too, need to work on. But what happens if we have this point of view, is that we will wait until we are alone with our significant other to ask the questions. And I'm sorry, but your husband probably doesn't know any more than you do. So, he now has to call up your advisor afterward and ask your question and then relay the message back to you. You know what I call this? The game of Telephone, where your question gets misconstrued and our answer gets all jumbled up. So, please speak up during your next meeting, and if you feel too intimidated, maybe your advisor isn't the right fit for you.

You want to work with someone who is approachable, trusting, and who you can have a conversation with about your deepest fears around money. I recently met with my good friend's mom, who manages all her family's finances. She and her husband have been working with the same advisor for over 30 years. After our session, she explained for the first time, that she was able to have a real conversation about her concerns with their pending retirement and what she really wanted to do once she is retired. She said she has never been able to talk with her current advisor like she had with me. Please find someone who really understands you and isn't afraid to ask you the tough questions, like "What will happen if you run out of money at age eighty?" Or someone who isn't scared to call you on your shit! We all need to stop tiptoeing around what the problem is; it isn't helping anyone. If your advisor is constantly saying you are fine without asking you any questions about your fears and concerns, something is wrong. You have been forewarned!

Our reactions are what we chose to live by in the present moment. We can decide to pass off managing our money again and again, or we can decide to take action and get involved. My new CFO of Your Life membership (different from my mentorship), is all about getting more involved. This is a monthly membership where you learn all the basics of creating the right financial foundation with your money and how to change your mindset around your money.

Remember the woman in my mentorship program I spoke about during the first chapter? Well, she recently came in, and we did some transformation on her mindset around money and people with money. She had all these negative emotions and connotations around money; she thought rich people were greedy, and she did not want to be greedy. If you feel rich people are bad and greedy, then you are sending yourself messages to not get rich. You are actually telling the universe you do not want more money. It took our entire meeting for her to start understanding she is repelling money instead of welcoming it into her life. Since our meeting, she's gotten her first referral check in the mail. She's made more money as she's changed her mindset, in addition to raising how she values herself.

Because I work for my father, I used to think I didn't deserve the money I made. I thought the rest of the world was thinking this way also. So, I didn't like to be flashy with my money or show it off at all. I was very concerned about what other people would think. That I don't work hard for it; that Daddy's giving me money because I'm his daughter, and on and on. I now know that is completely ridiculous since I have the proof of how hard I've worked and am working now. But there was a part of my brain always saying, *you don't deserve to make this money*. Because I've changed my mindset around it, I've earned more money the past four months consistently. It's amazing how a little shift in our mindset can transform our lives.

Usually, we don't even know we are risking our money with our subliminal messages. If you don't really want a specific job, it comes across during your job interview. Even if you thought you dominated the interview, you were holding back in some way since you really didn't want it. The membership goes into detail about how our mindset affects money coming into and going out of our lives. We use it in tandem with a lot of financial content, so you not only learn it, but you will also learn how to implement it to take your life to the next level. And more importantly, you will learn how to change our reactions to positive ones and keep our lives moving in the right direction.

The woman whose husband passed away is still living in the past, and not moving her life forward. You won't be like her; you will choose to live for today and for tomorrow, NOT for yesterday. She isn't helping her children by avoiding her money. She isn't teaching them how to manage and value their money, and what happens if she loses her brother? Will she just pass the torch to her child? If she does, she will always be dependent on someone else for her money. You are here to become INDEPENDENT, not dependent on your money, so I know you will keep making the right shifts in your life to gain control and confidence with your money.

Ask yourself, how will you react to the next hurdle in your life?

- Negatively

- Angry

- Avoid it

- Emotionally

- Positively

- Embrace it and grow from it

During your next storm cloud, write down one saying you will repeat to react positively to it immediately:

_____

_____

Write down one task you will do to react positively to it within a day of it happening:

_____

_____

Write down your actions with your money for the next:

Week:_____

Month:_____

1 Year:_____

5 Years:_____

Chapter 7: Are You Proud of the Woman in the Mirror?

"I'm proud of the woman I am today because I went through one hell of a time becoming her." ~Unknown

You should be proud of yourself for making it to chapter 7 and for all you have already implemented from reading this book. It's not always easy, but as we start to see the small changes in our lives, it makes it worth it. As I've shifted my life to get more satisfaction and happiness from my work, it has spilled over into all the areas of my life. I care less about making tons of money, even though I am making more money. I don't need high-end designer handbags to feel successful because the more women I'm able to transform, the more success I feel. I'm able to be excited for other people's triumphs whereas before, I would have been jealous. I'm happier at home, more at peace, and a lot less anxious, as well as I embrace life's new challenges because I know they will only move me closer to my dreams.

Take a few moments to reflect on what your changes have done for your life. Have those around you started to take notice, started to change how they act toward you, or maybe they don't like seeing you move forward? There will always be people in our lives who want to keep us still, so they don't feel bad about their life. Those people are not worth your time! You want to be around people who are as ambitious and inspired as you are to level up your life because they will keep you on the right path and will be there to lift you up if you fall. I will be there for you if you stumble, too. I will help you refocus and get you to move forward even if it's just a few tiptoes at first. Build your support system with people like us. It really does make a world of a difference when you do.

I can tell you it does from my own experience. As I told you earlier, I am working with a coach, and she put together a mentorship for women entrepreneurs. There are 14 of us, highly ambitious and motivated women who really want to make a difference in the world and for the right reasons. When I am tired and feel stuck, these women are the ones who pull me up and push me forward. They all inspire me, and I hope at times, I get to repay the favor. We are all completely open and honest with our successes and failures. We are very raw with each other since it doesn't help if you hide what is working and what isn't working.

As women, we like to hide our weaknesses and failures, and probably over-exaggerate our victories. We are too guarded to be completely open with each other about a lot of our lives. How many times have you been surprised to hear about someone's divorce, someone's illness, or that they have lost their job? Too many times, since we all want each other to think everything is FINE, everything is OK. You don't want to share with your girlfriend about your mounting debt, yet you still agree to go out to fancy restaurants and get your nails done with her, to put up a front that everything is FINE. Why do we feel the need to MASK our lives with the ones we love the most? It even pertains to our parents; we want them to always think we've made it and are big successes. They know about life, and all the ups and downs. The ups and downs are what make us who we are, so why do we always have to hide them?

I just had a strategy session with a young woman, who desperately wants to move out of her parent's house. To her, this will make her parents proud, and she will feel like a success and an adult. Problem is, her parents have drilled into her head how important it is to save, and she won't be able to save if she moves out. She's scared if she moves out, but then has to move back in with mom and dad one day, that it would make her a disappointment. She's put all these limiting beliefs on herself, which explains why she is terrified to go out on her own. Yet she wants it so badly; she is ready to do anything. First, we are getting her past her limiting beliefs that she can't afford to move out. We are tracking her money, and we are reprioritizing her wants so she can. Her goal is to be out in a few months, and I'm sure we will hit that goal!

I know it is a HUGE faux pas to talk about our money with anyone besides our significant other, accountant, and financial advisor. But can I ask if we can throw that misperception out the window like we did with wearing white pants after Labor Day? The problem with never talking about it is, we never know how we are actually doing. How am I doing? That's the very first question I get from 99 percent of the people who work with me. The people who are a little behind in their goals usually think they are further ahead, and those who are in good shape think they are in terrible shape. We never know how we are doing because we can't talk about it! By not talking about it and by not knowing how we are doing, it only adds to our stress. Try to be open and honest with your loved ones; it will free up a lot of your stress.

One woman I just met with kept reiterating how she would compare herself repeatedly to her friends. I instantly told her to stop comparing herself to her friends. Trust me; she isn't the first woman I've heard this from either. Heck, I'm guilty of it, too! I explained that the only person she can compare herself to is herself three months ago. This is why I strongly believe we need to have more open communication about our money; I feel it is a dangerous and horrible road to take if you start comparing yourself. There will always be someone with more money, a bigger house, nicer vacations, and more cars. No one makes the same amount of money, nor do we all want the same things. You don't have the same amount of money as your best friend, but you also don't have the same goals. Your idea of success isn't her idea of success. One person wants a high paying job to feel like they've made it whereas, someone else wants a low-stress job with much lower pay. Both people are happy and satisfied with their work even though they live very different lifestyles.

Knowing what it is you really want in your life is key to your motivation, but also to how you view your success. This is why I had you identify it first in our journey together. Your sister might buy a brand-new BMW, and now you can be happy for her and not jealous because what you really want is a secure retirement, not a new luxury car. I was terrible with jealousy when I was younger. I would think *they don't deserve that like I do; they didn't work hard for it.* Instead of thinking, *they can get that nice house, and that means we can, too.* The women in my mentorship taught me more about shifting my mindset to feel joy for those who obtain their goals because it means I can obtain my goals, too. If they can get such great results, I can as well. It keeps me moving toward my goals.

Now that you've made leaps and bounds with your mindset, money, and life, let's take a moment to look back. I'm going to **gift** you with one more motivational activity to complete before you finish this book and your transformation. The activity was created by my new friend Kyra, who has an amazing new business called Monkey Bread[7].

---

[7]*Monkey Bread is not affiliated with or endorsed by Raymond James.*

Monkey Bread is a monthly membership, where Kyra will send you an activity each month.

The purpose of the task is to bring you back to your childhood and to simpler times. So, to get you ready, I want you to go to a quiet place where you can be by yourself and comfortable.

Grab a piece of paper or if you like technology—your smartphone.

Take a look at the little girl in the picture. She's a cutie, isn't she? Envision the little girl is you, and she is on the phone with the present you. She starts asking you some questions as all little children do. *Is your favorite color still purple? Do you still like Mom's apple pie the most?* And some harder questions, such as *are you happy? Did you fulfill all our dreams? Do you love what you do? Are we rich?* I threw the last one in for fun. Rich to a little girl might be 10 dollars. The reason for the last question is to determine how you define rich in your life now, at this moment. Is it still $5 million or is it to feel safe and secure with your money? Is it to be able to provide and help your family when they really need it? To go for your dream job that you will LOVE? So, when she asks you these questions, what will you say?

How many of your little girl dreams have you achieved?

_____

_____

_____

Are you happy?

_____

_____

_____

Do you love where you are in your life right now?

_____

_____

_____

Are you rich and what does being rich mean to you now?

_____

_____

_____

We are our toughest critic, yet we can be the most open and honest with ourselves. So, be honest with your childhood self, and don't worry if you haven't done everything you set out to do when you were eight. As we grow, our goals will change, and we will get new ones. Of course, you aren't an astronaut, just as I am not the first woman who made it to the NBA, but what are the dreams you do want to make happen?

What is left on your list? Let's get them done, so you won't wind up talking to yourself again in another 20 years apologizing for never going for your dream when you had the chance. Prove to your younger self you are a strong, confident, and secure woman, who will take action to make her dream a reality. Remember, your life is worth it, and maybe you need to tell yourself that, but more importantly, you need to start to believe it. You borrowed my belief at the beginning of this book, but now you know it for yourself.

If I had done this exercise three years ago, it would have been difficult. I would have lied to my younger self in pigtails because it would have been too difficult to say. "I hate my job." I had a great family life with my now amazing husband and dog; I had great friends and family, but my career felt like it was going nowhere. It would have been very hard to admit this to myself, and I never even realized it until I was on the other side where I enjoy going to work every day, so much so, that I don't want to leave at the end of the day.

You can picture yourself in the future, now waving at you from the other side of a field. She is the woman you want to be, who you are working toward becoming. All the work you've put into reading this book comprises your steps to getting there, to this woman you want to be. As we finish our journey together, keep moving toward her, and if you feel like you are moving farther away from her, I can help. Build your plan; get your strategies in place; implement and take action, and always remember: **YOU are worth it**. You are worth getting out of debt. You are worth asking for a raise and promotion. You are worth saving for the retirement you want.

You are worth it.

Fill in what you are worth:

_____

_____

_____

Remember why you are doing all that you are: to get to a new and better place. It takes time, energy, and strength to do what you are embarking on. The woman, I interviewed and told you about at the start of this book couldn't wait to tell me her story. Remember, she was a stay-at-home mother of three daughters, the youngest one under a year old when her husband left her for another family. The reason she couldn't wait to tell me about what she had been through was because she is now a successful teacher with three amazing daughters, a loving boyfriend, and about to retire. The steps she took to get there weren't easy, and she leaned on a lot of family for support. She made up new traditions with her girls, went back to school, and created a new and better life for them.

Sharing these stories with more women can help spread the word that women are stronger than we think, and we need to give ourselves more credit than we do. I love working with women like the ones I've mentioned, who are ready to take action, and who take new steps in their lives. I can always light a fire under your ass if you need, but if I want it more for you than you want it for yourself, you won't get the results. We need to both be committed to your transformation because trust me when you finally reach the other side of the field, it will all be worth it.

It's just like losing weight. If it was easy, we would all be skinny; if getting out of debt or saving money was a snap, we would all be rich. It isn't easy. It's tough work, and it takes time. If you got out of debt in one day after being in debt for years, most likely, you will fall right back into your old patterns of debt. If you saved $1 million in a month, chances are you'll spend it in a month as well. The time and energy it takes creates a stronger commitment and makes the satisfaction so much greater. Oh, how you will feel once you get there! I'm beyond thrilled for you to feel what it is like when you start crossing those dreams off your checklist, living them, and creating more. That feeling of accomplishment is subpar to only a handful of other goals. I want you to have that feeling again. And this brings us to our last chapter together.

Chapter 8: Why Is the Asset You Are Working Toward Driving Your Change?

"She builds others up because she knows what it's like to be torn down." ~Unknown

We are winding down our journey together, and you should celebrate all the progress you have made with your money, your mindset, your life, and your family's life. You will likely start to see how the changes you have made with your finances will impact other areas of your life. It is incredible to witness the other ways you will see change. I can say this firsthand since I've seen it for myself.

As I start changing the reasons why I work so hard to help transform more women's lives, I find I care less about the material things in life. Before, I thought it was all about making more money because that is what success meant to me. But now, it is about the impact I can make on women's lives. This change also affected how I spend money; I now give more to charity; I care less about designer clothes and handbags, and truly appreciate what I already have so much more. My husband and I sponsor a child in Guatemala, and it is such a reality check when our small monthly donation can completely change his family's entire life. Being able to take on more sponsor children to improve their lives and their family's lives is so much more rewarding than buying a new handbag. And I love to give back to organizations, which help animals, especially dogs. By helping more women, I'm able to help more animals and dogs find good homes, and that feeling is unbeatable.

How has your new mindset affected other areas around you? Have other people noticed yet? If they haven't, it is only a matter of time. It will create a ripple effect from what you are doing. One of my one-on-one clients was in my office the other day, and I had her go through an exercise where we drew out 10 steps, one leading to the next. We started at the bottom, and I asked what money means to her. At the bottom of her set of stairs, she put: "Money is a tool to live the life I want." After taking some time to dig a LOT deeper, at the top of her set of stairs she had: "Money allows me to help improve the lives around me." The focus moved from her to everyone in her life. She is no longer changing just for herself. She is changing for those around her, and this is much more powerful.

Just as negative people can bring those around them down, positive people can bring others up. It is your choice to decide which type of person you want to be, either a good influence on your loved ones or a poor one. If you are in debt and are working to get out of it, those around you will notice. You will inspire them to make changes, too. If you start to make saving a priority to get to your goals, you will motivate others to do so as well. They don't want to be left behind while you have your dream retirement; they want it too. And when they start working toward it, then the people around them will change. This is what I mean by the quote at the beginning of the chapter: **"She builds others up because she knows what it's like to be torn down."**

Before we come to an end, let's take a moment to review all you've accomplished throughout this book.

In Chapter 2, we decided why we are transforming our lives. What is our reason? Always remember your reason. It will get you through the hard times and make the good times that much better. Remember what accomplishment feels like? When was the last time you felt it? It is a feeling like no other, and you need to take in the emotion that is created from truly accomplishing something incredible. I want you to have that feeling again and know why you are working so hard. I will continue to work with you to help you achieve more and more. Embrace these accomplishments, celebrate them, and use them to keep going.

In Chapter 3, we identified our old money stories, and whether they are jeopardizing our future goals and ambitions. We learned about our spending triggers or "bad decision triggers" and found a way to prevent them from ruining our lives. And lastly, we created our new money mantras, which are our new money beliefs and the ways to live by. Use your money mantra as your positive affirmation every day to propel you forward.

In the 4th chapter, we learned how to take action in our lives by first making the decision that our life is worth changing. Next, we need to gain clarity, so we will know the direction we want to go in. And finally, we must implement and be accountable. Otherwise, we will never get there. You wrote down your top life goals and your top money goals, which are the first steps in holding yourself accountable. Keep your goals top of mind and go through them every month.

In Chapter 5, it was all about building your plan, and the various financial components to think about when you do. Where are your weaknesses? Where are your strengths, and will you know when it is time to outsource it to a professional? It is your life after all and your life savings. Don't you think it is worth it to spend some time and money with a professional to make sure you are on the right track? I can help show you where it makes sense to utilize a professional, and I can be that professional for you, too. There are many ways I work with people, whether it is one-on-one coaching, as an advisor, or in my monthly membership program. When you outsource, it shouldn't cost you extra time or money, and it needs to make sense for your situation, as well as potentially end up saving you time, money, and a lot of stress and frustration. You can read more about how to get involved in my world in the About the Author Chapter.

We found out how our reactions dictate how our lives will be lived in Chapter 6; that we can choose to react positively and embrace change or negatively, and get stuck in the past forever.

Chapter 7 is about the woman you are today, and the woman you want to become. Who do you want to look back at you when you stare into the mirror? Life is built on choices, and it is your choice now.

My goal in writing this book is to make you also rethink the meaning of ASSETS in the title. By now, the term "assets" shouldn't just describe money to you. "Assets" is whatever it is you are working for, whether it is more: happiness, security, time with your family, freedom, peace of mind, job satisfaction, etc. I want to know what the asset is that you are working for. My asset is transforming more women's lives by helping them feel more secure and confident with their money. What is yours? I'd love to hear what assets meant to you when you started the book and what they mean to you now. Email https://www.jessicaweaver.com/contact.

your meaning, and you could be showcased in my next book.

I notice this transformation more and more when I start working with people. At first, people are all about earning more money, growing their money, and saving more money. As you can tell, it is money, money, money. But by the end of the conversation, I am able to open them up a little more and get to the core of it. For grandparents, it is about leaving their grandchildren money for college or for their wedding, to be able to leave their legacy. For new parents, it is about peace of mind if something happens to one of them. For a divorced mom, it is about confidence with her new life and her desire to gain control over her money. For a woman starting out, it is about the security they can have the life they want while paying down student loans, enjoying their life, and being independent. At every new transition in life, you can see our assets or goals will change.

Your life won't stop once you hit your first goal; you will find new ones to go after. For that exact reason, I write about all life stages for women. Because even if you aren't near retirement yet, you will be one day. One of the most enjoyable parts of my job is to see the women I work with hit their goals, create new ones, and continue their journey through life. Seeing them buy a house, have children, have a successful career, retire, and enjoy their grandchildren is so fulfilling. I don't just work with my clients for a small part of their lives; I strive to work with them for their entire life, their children's lives, and their grandchildren's lives. They become a part of our family, and our goal with anyone new we are working with is to build a long and lasting relationship. They are always calling us to tell us their child got engaged, sending us pictures of their babies, and sharing the blueprint of their new house. It really is a joy to be with them through these stages and better yet, to help them get to the stages.

As you progress into becoming the person you want to be and are proud of, your critter brain will creep up. Whenever we start seeing any type of success, we tend to second-guess it. Remember you are making some major shifts in your life, and change is scary, so we might try to sabotage our own success. When we start earning more money, we think *am I really worth that amount of money? Am I getting paid more than I'm worth? What if I don't deliver?* When we get out of debt, we usually find ourselves back into debt very quickly because that is how we have always lived and how we have valued our lives. The purpose of this book is to help get you past these limiting beliefs and for you to start valuing yourself so you can live the life you want and reach your goals.

I started my blog, *Not Your Father's Advisor*, in June of 2016, and was so excited to reach 100 views. Then the views started to climb higher, and I was thrilled because I was starting to make a major impact on women I'd never even met before. In the fall of 2016, I hit 500 views, and thought *wow, I'm really doing it*! My goal was to hit 1,000 by April of 2017, and I admit I was nervous I wouldn't make it. And then in January, I hit 2,000 with one of my favorite posts about women empowering themselves to transform their lives. In March, another post about women becoming the family caretaker hit 3,000 and then 6,000, and amazingly, over 11,500 in one week. I was shocked by the huge increase in views, but then my critter brain came in and said *it won't last. It's a fluke.* But guess what happened in the next two weeks? I was averaging between 9,000 and 10,000 views, so NO to my critter brain. It **wasn't** a fluke.

With the number of people reading my blog, I started to second-guess myself. *Am I so good that 10,000 people want to read my blog*? When all year long, I'd never doubted the value I'd provided. I'd always felt very proud of the content I'd written, knew it was a fun, different, and interesting perspective I provide to my readers. I KNEW it was only a matter of time for it to take off. Yet, when it took off, I started second-guessing it. Why? It was what I wanted, to be able to reach more and more women, so why did I doubt it? It was so much change so quickly; it was hard to process it. And this may happen with you as well. But remember, you ARE worth it, and you DO deserve it. You've worked hard for it and will continue to work hard because isn't it all worth it in the end? If you are like the women I work with and will only work with, the answer is YES. If the answer is no, I probably won't work with you. I only want to work with women who want to transform their life as much as I want it for them. They are the ones who will be committed, who will take action, and implement.

If you know you fit my criteria, let's talk and see how you can get involved in my world. My promise to you is that I will do ANYTHING to change your life, and my commitment is to always be there for you before, during, and after. I won't just tell you what to do or why you should do it. More importantly, I will show you how to do it. I won't just talk AT you without listening; I will be talking WITH you. Most financial advisors just tell you some facts, give you some suggestions, and send you on your way. Not me, remember I'm *Not Your Father's Advisor*, after all.

As you can tell from all the stories I've shared throughout this book, I care very deeply for the women who work with me. The greatest pleasure is seeing how they've transformed their lives with just some tweaks and modifications along with having an accountability partner.

To see the first woman I wrote about in this book start earning more money because she values her life more is unbelievable. From raising her life's value, she has been able to understand her worth, charge more money, put some much-needed focus back on herself, and invest in herself. When people decide to work with me, I believe they are really deciding to invest in their own life. And what better investment is there than yourself?

How about the woman who kept getting support from her parents? She decided to invest in herself as well. By finally deciding enough was enough, she won't live in debt anymore or depend on mom and dad; she chose to believe her life was worth more than that. She became stronger through the process of working with me and realized her "asset" is more financial security and no more money stress. Since sharing her story, she's updated me that she's gotten a bonus from work.

She's saved more money and is now earning more money, which is just the icing on the cake compared to the security and confidence she now feels. Her parents are proud of her, her children are even more proud of her, and she is the proudest because she did it, with my help, I will add. The tools I gave her, I won't take away, she can use them indefinitely throughout her life. She's gone from complete embarrassment, and non-stop stress, and fear with her money situation to financial security all within a few months.

And my good friend, who got divorced and has found a happier and better way to live? She came out stronger and more independent than before and is more secure with her money, too. She isn't more secure because she is making more money or spending less, but because she gained knowledge about it. She better understands how it works, where before, she'd just agreed to whatever her husband said to do with it. She took control over her finances, her life, and her happiness.

Lastly, the woman who finally decided to quit the corporate world (which only left her exhausted and stressed), and who went on to her retirement. She gained one of the most crucial things for her life, clarity. She took action and instead of being chained to a job she hated, she changed her lifestyle so she could retire and more importantly stay retired. She found out what she wanted more than the high-paying job, nice wardrobe, and big house, and it was financial security.

Security that she can have the retirement she wants with family, friends, travel, and lots of experiences.

What do all these women, who have made huge transformations have in common?

- They made a decision.

- They took action despite feeling scared, nervous, or stuck.

- They implemented and stayed accountable. AND

- They did all happen to work with me, or someone they knew who wanted it as much as they did. They used an accountability partner, someone they trusted, who would push them and would be there for them no matter what.

This is what I live for, and why I am on this earth. I kept praying to be shown how to make an impact in life. I've made leaps and bounds to get to this point, to be able to touch more women's lives through my work, through my blog, and now with this book. I've put in the late nights, worked weekends, and invested in myself because I knew I could make a difference. And I will continue to work my butt off to be there for you and more women. This is my promise to you.

Every woman in this book, myself included, had a different journey. Their journey might not work for you, and your journey might not work for someone else. But I made examples of their stories to show you that it can happen, so they have been included to help build the belief in you. All it takes is a decision.

So, what will be your decision? It's in your hands now.

About the Author

Jessica grew up in Hunterdon County, New Jersey with her parents, older brother, and the family's standard poodle, Inky. She was a quiet and shy child, who quickly took to sports, of which she played a variety. But her passion has always been basketball. Since her father played basketball in college, they bonded over their joint love for the sport. Jess had very low self-esteem and playing sports allowed her to find her voice. Since she was such a shy child with a lack of confidence, Jess now finds it rewarding to get people to open up about their finances and concerns around their money. People tend to be very guarded when it comes to their financial situation. Knowing how detrimental it can be to hide away and avoid talking, she is able to get them to be more honest in the telling of their stories.

She remembers clinging to her mother during birthday parties and other occasions with a lot of children around. Ironically, people cling the same way to their money, and by helping people identify their true money concerns, she helps them transform their lives. If we always stay on the surface, we really aren't helping anyone.

Jessica went to a small private high school, Rutgers Prep, to follow her dreams of playing basketball one day in college. She loved the diverse environment of the high school, especially after being in Catholic school for nine years, where the most diverse you got was an Irish Catholic and an Italian Catholic. She had four great years there, received an amazing education, and was a part of five state champion teams. She was recruited to play basketball and run cross country in college, but as you know, her passion was basketball. Besides, she hated running, though she would later get back to running after college. She committed to playing basketball at another small school, Moravian College in Bethlehem, PA.

At Moravian, Jessica became a part of the women's basketball team, and knew immediately the women she played with would be her lifelong friends. Being trapped on a bus for hours at a time on the way to games, really makes you bond on a new level. You go through the ups and downs of a season that always seems so long when you're playing, but once it is over, you miss it every day. Being with these amazing, inspiring, and extremely competitive women is a big reason Jess loves working with women. She understands the bond between women when times are tough, but also when it is time to celebrate each other's victories.

Besides the lifelong friends Jess made at college, she studied economics and business management to get ready for her life after basketball. She fell in love with economics and decided to major in it while minoring in management. Jess met her now-husband in college; he was the same year and was in her first-class freshman year, Spanish. Eric was also on the men's basketball team and a great athlete and person overall.

As you can tell, it is destined for their children to play basketball. They started dating in the spring of sophomore year, and the rest is history.

Since Jess is quite competitive, she found it hard at times to be happy for her teammate's successes. And there were a lot of them! She played with 5 1,000-point scorers and was a 1,000-point scorer both in college and high school herself. She played with 3 All Americans, and participated in and witnessed countless other record-breaking moments with her teammates.

When we see other people getting bonuses, promotions, and buying newer and bigger houses, we tend to get jealous, too. Instead of viewing their success as positive, we get mad they received it, and we didn't. We should think, *if they can reach that milestone, I can, too.* There are plenty of points, rebounds, and records to break, just as there is plenty of money in this world to make. If your neighbor is earning an extra $100,000 each year, it doesn't mean there is $100,000 less in this world for you.

Throughout this book and in her blog, *Not Your Father's Advisor*, Jess references mindset and positive thinking. She is more mindset-focused than your typical advisor, and it all started when she was in college. She was such a maniac about basketball and would allow her negative thinking to get the better of her, so it affected her performance on the court. Jess decided to make a change and started seeing a sports psychologist to help her enjoy playing again. It did wonders for her during her junior year, and because of the impact she saw firsthand, she has gone back to it in her work. It always amazes Jess when she sees the mental shift in people and how it affects other areas of their lives.

After college, Jess joined her father and brother at her father's financial firm. She and her brother took their licensing exams in the summer of 2010, started studying for their CERTIFIED FINANCIAL PLANNER™ designation in 2011, and passed in 2012. While Jess never thought about how her life's path had brought her to the moment of writing her book, throughout her life, there were big moments that led her to that place. It wasn't just because her father is a financial advisor, and she wanted to continue the bond they had from basketball, although that was part of it. Working with women, getting people to be less shy about their money, helping them to change their mindset and beliefs surrounding money all pointed her to where she is now.

Jess resides in Morris County with her husband, Eric, and their dachshund, Duke. She is an active runner in a running club at the shore, and she loves to run half-marathons, especially. Eric and Jess love to travel and experience new places, so much so that every anniversary they surprise each other with a trip. They alternate years for who gets to plan the excursion, something she highly recommends doing. They are expecting their first child in September of 2017 (who they just found out is a GIRL) and hopefully, will have a few more if you ask Jess.

If you want to learn more about how to get involved in Jess's world, read below:

There are a couple of different ways Jess works with her clients.

She takes on the traditional role of a financial advisor, where she manages her client's money and creates an overall financial plan for them. In this capacity, she reviews all aspects of finances, including estate plans, insurance review, cash flow management, investments, savings strategies, and so much more. Jess also creates long-lasting relationships with her clients and is there for them when times are rough or when there are moments to celebrate. Last year, she helped a couple celebrate their sixty-fifth wedding anniversary. She has also been present for ten retirements, and countless babies and grandbabies. She is proud to say she is one of the first people her clients call to share their good news, and on the flip side, her clients are comfortable telling her when times are tough. Jess plans to work with all her clients for the rest of their lives, their children's lives, and their grandchildren's lives.

While she enjoys working as an advisor, there are times when her clients need more one-on-one time to really make an impact. If someone has debilitating money beliefs and behaviors, Jess has created a 6-month program to help people transform their relationship with money and to make it work more effectively for their lives and their goals. Jess started noticing how people seem to think the work is done once they get their financial plan in place, but then they don't make any progress. Even though their money issues are addressed during the plan, they aren't taught how to change them. Jess saw this as a huge problem, and it is why she started to learn more and research how to be a money coach versus just an advisor. The other reason she has created this new part of her business is because typically advisors will work with only those who have assets for them to manage. There are so many people who need guidance and help with their money, but who don't have enough saved up to pay an advisor to work with them. They still need help and guidance, so Jess found a way to give it to them.

To get on Jess's calendar to see if you are the right fit to work with her, schedule your 10-minute call on the website below:

https://www.jessicaweaver.com/contact